SOURDOUGH
EVERY DAY

SOURDOUGH
EVERY DAY

Your Guide to Using Active and Discard Starter for
Artisan Bread, Rolls, Pasta, Sweets *and More*

HANNAH DELA CRUZ

Saveur Award Winner and Founder of Make It Dough

Photography by Gaby J.

PAGE STREET
PUBLISHING CO.

PAGE STREET
PUBLISHING CO.

First published in 2020 by
Page Street Publishing Co.
27 Congress Street, Suite 105
Salem, MA 01970
www.pagestreetpublishing.com

Distributed by Macmillan, sales in Canada by The Canadian Manda Group.

24   23   22   3 4 5

ISBN-13: 978-1-64567-202-9

ISBN-10: 1-64567-202-6

Library of Congress Control Number: 2019957404

Cover by Rosie Stewart and book design by Meghan Baskis for Page Street Publishing Co.
Photography by Gaby J.

Printed and bound in the United States

TO JOEL

FOR GIVING ME THE FREEDOM TO FIND MY PASSION

CONTENTS

INTRODUCTION

I think you have to be obsessed with bread to be a baker.
—Nancy Silverton

I'm not a chef or a trained baker, but I am obsessed with bread. I fell fast and hard for sourdough. From the moment I created my first sourdough starter, I couldn't get enough. I loved the tactile nature of making bread; digging my hands into sticky dough and scoring loaves with beautiful patterns helped all my anxieties flow away. Soon I went from not eating bread for years to making several loaves a week to baking things I never thought would come out of my oven.

The moment I discovered sourdough, I found myself starving for information. I took in everything I could find. I read blogs, watched videos, collected cookbooks, consulted with strangers in Facebook groups and message boards, made friends on Instagram, even read research papers, just so I could understand exactly why my breads were not turning out the way I wanted them to. I needed to understand what was going on in my starter and how it was affecting my dough. I needed to know exactly why sourdough is good for you. And I needed to be able to answer people when they asked me, "What's the point of spending two days just to make one loaf of bread?"

Sourdough for me represents eliminating the phrase "I can't" from my vocabulary. I never thought I would be able to make bread. Once I did, I was no longer intimidated by anything else. This may sound dramatic, but sourdough changed my life.

Sourdough is transformative. Creating bread from just three ingredients—flour, water and salt—is nothing short of alchemy. The health benefits of sourdough are directly correlated with the length of time it takes to create a loaf. Natural yeasts present in sourdough act as an external stomach, predigesting the flour, which makes it easier for us to digest and allows our bodies to absorb nutrients that are normally locked away in wheat. In addition, the extended fermentation period allows the bread to develop deep, complex flavors that cannot be attained when you're using commercial yeast.

In the hopes of making sense of all the information I was learning, as well as to document my progress by sharing the recipes I had created, I started the blog MakeItDough.com. A year later, I found myself on stage at the *Saveur* Magazine Blog Awards accepting the 2019 prize for Most Obsessive Blog. Today, more than 10,000 people have joined me on my journey through Instagram and thousands of people visit my blog each day. I've received hundreds of messages from home bakers like me who have successfully re-created my recipes.

This book is a product of my *passion* for sourdough. I'll teach you everything I know about successfully creating an active sourdough culture in a way that is not too obsessive or cumbersome.

The first 20 recipes I've created for you (from Beginner's Sourdough Bread [page 20] to Sesame–Poppy Seed Barbari Bread [page 81]) use sourdough for its magical fermenting and leavening abilities to create delicious breads. The remaining recipes (starting with Whole Wheat Roti [page 82]) make use of sourdough discarded during the feeding process in deliciously unexpected ways, including dumpling wrappers for Pork-Ginger Gyoza (page 97), Piña Colada Upside Down Cake (page 138), Flour Tortillas (page 85) and Moroccan-Inspired Chicken Empanadas (page 166).

The recipes in this book are not for a large crowd, because I usually bake for just myself and my boyfriend. If you're baking for a large group, though, these recipes can easily be doubled.

Before we embark on this journey together, I'd like to thank you for picking this book from among so many others to guide you on your very own adventure.

Hannahmae Dela Cruz

LET'S GET STARTED

Bread is the greatest alchemy of all. —Michael Pollan

I'm so glad you've decided to begin your sourdough journey with me. In this chapter, I'll explain everything you need to get started to create your very first loaf of bread, including how to make your own sourdough starter. I'll introduce you to some breadmaking techniques and the terminology you'll come across throughout this book. And most importantly, I'll share the tips I've learned throughout my own adventure with sourdough.

Perhaps the most important tip for beginners is to purchase and use a kitchen scale to weigh your ingredients, measuring them in grams instead of cups. Grams are far more accurate and less subjective than cups and will help you achieve the most consistent results in your baking.

I've provided the ingredient measurements first in grams throughout all my recipes to encourage you to use grams while baking your way through this book.

CREATING YOUR SOURDOUGH STARTER

Sourdough starter is a miracle in a jar. It's a thriving ecosystem of yeast and bacteria living in perfect harmony—one that, if cared for, can even outlive you. There is a fair amount of complicated science involved in a sourdough starter, and it's nice to understand all the interactions within it, but you don't need a PhD to make great bread. The only thing you need to keep in mind is that to create beautiful bread, you'll need a mature, active starter that can produce enough carbon dioxide (bubbles) to make bread rise. You will never produce a good loaf of bread using a weak starter.

For all its complexity, creating a sourdough starter could not be simpler. All you need is flour, water, a jar, time and, perhaps the most important ingredient of all, patience. Nurturing a strong starter takes time—about two weeks. Using your starter before it has matured is an exercise in futility that will result in a dense loaf, frustration and wasted time and ingredients.

The great thing is you'll only have to undertake this process once. After your starter has matured, you can use it forever.

In the process of harvesting and nurturing a sourdough culture, you'll need to discard all but a very small portion of your starter. The concept of throwing away a large part of your starter can be quite bewildering for beginners. But there is a method to the madness. As the microscopic organisms in your starter build strength and multiply to create a symbiotic culture of bacteria and yeast, these yeast need to feed on flour and water. But if the yeast population is too large, it will require an unmanageable amount of flour and water to survive. Because you'll have to throw away a lot of the starter when you begin this process, my method of creating a starter uses a very small amount of flour and water. Through my experience, I've found that this method is considerably less wasteful but is still enough to kickstart a very healthy, active culture.

To avoid food waste, I've created tons of delicious and creative ways to use the starter you remove—what we call sourdough discard. Once your starter has matured, you'll be able to store the discard indefinitely in your refrigerator to make any of the sourdough discard recipes in this book.

SOURDOUGH STARTER

A Mason jar works well for making sourdough starter, but any glass jar with a screw-on lid will do. Don't be too worried about sterilizing your jar or tools. Just make sure that everything you use is clean and free of any soap residue. Remember, nurturing sourdough is an ancient tradition that existed long before bleach. Once your starter has matured, it will be able to ward off any mold or harmful bacteria.

DAY 1

14 g (1 tbsp) water

14 g (2 tbsp) all-purpose or whole wheat flour

1 (8- to 12-oz [240- to 355-ml]) glass jar

Combine the water and flour in the jar and stir until they are fully mixed. You'll want all the flour to be thoroughly incorporated. Screw on the lid and set the jar aside in a warm spot in your kitchen where you won't forget about it. If you'd like, stick a piece of tape on your jar and mark the date you started it.

DAYS 2 TO 3

Once a day, open the jar and use a spoon to stir your starter. You may not see very many changes in it on day 2, but you'll notice that the mixture has started to transform from a thick paste into something that resembles the consistency of yogurt.

On day 3, you'll be able to see more signs of fermentation. The smell will change and you'll start seeing bubbles in the mixture. But don't be too worried if you don't see a lot of activity.

Day 1: Throughout the day, your starter will transform from a dry dough to a substance that resembles a thick yogurt.

Days 2 to 3: You'll begin to see a few bubbles form in your starter and its aroma will start to change, taking on a fermented smell similar to cheese. Your starter may experience a burst of activity as yeast fights for dominance in your culture.

DAY 4

14 g (2 tbsp) all-purpose or whole wheat flour

14 g (1 tbsp) water

At this point, your starter should appear more active and look a little bit more liquefied, with more bubbles distributed throughout. Add the flour and water and stir until they are fully combined. Screw on the lid and set the jar aside.

You can choose any type of flour to make your sourdough starter. Personally, I've found my starter works best when fed with all-white unbleached bread flour, so the recipes in this book use this type of starter. You can also change the type of flour you feed your starter at any point in this process. The yeast in your starter will need a few feedings to adjust to its new food source, but it won't cause any harm. Some people even create and maintain starters made with gluten-free flours—although I won't be covering that topic in this book.

Day 4: Your starter may liquefy, indicating that it is hungry and needs to be fed. Follow the feeding instructions and set your starter aside.

Days 5 to 9: Your starter may appear flat and experience a lull in activity during this period. The smell will change drastically and may be a bit off-putting, but this is completely normal.

Days 10 to 14 (Unfed): As your starter builds strength it will begin to smell sweeter, resembling the aroma of beer or yogurt. Even before feeding, the texture will appear spongy.

Days 10 to 14 (Fed): An active starter will double or triple in volume in 4 to 6 hours and will have an even distribution of large bubbles throughout. At this stage, your starter will be strong enough to make bread rise.

DAYS 5 TO 9

30 g (2 tbsp) water

30 g (¼ cup) all-purpose or whole wheat flour

At this stage, natural yeasts in your sourdough culture are beginning to build strength, so you'll have to start feeding them once a day. The feeding process is quite straightforward, but it can be confusing for beginners.

1. Throw away all but 14 grams (about 1 tablespoon) of sourdough starter.

2. Stir 30 grams (2 tablespoons) of water and 30 grams (¼ cup) of flour into the remaining sourdough starter.

3. Seal the jar and set it aside.

4. Repeat this process every day for five days.

You don't have to be obsessive about feeding your starter at an exact time each day. I've found that as long as you feed it every day around the same time (for example, any time in the morning or right before bed), you'll be able to nurture a strong, active culture.

I don't advise keeping any of the discard to bake with at this point, because your starter hasn't developed the optimum acidity or built a community of healthy yeast and good bacteria.

During this period, your starter could go through different stages of activity. Because each culture is unique, it can be difficult to predict what your starter will look like. It could literally explode with activity, or it might appear dormant. *Don't let a lull in activity discourage you.* Continue feeding your starter daily and it will eventually gain strength and mature. Remember, unless you cook your starter or it grows mold, it is not dead.

DAYS 10 TO 14

30 g (2 tbsp) water

30 g (¼ cup) all-purpose or whole wheat flour

Starting on day 10, you will need to begin feeding your starter twice each day, leaving about 8 to 12 hours between feedings. To make the process simple for myself, I usually feed my starter in the morning when I wake up and in the evening after I eat dinner.

During every feeding, discard all but 14 grams (about 1 tablespoon) of the sourdough starter. Add 30 grams (2 tablespoons) of water and 30 grams (¼ cup) of flour to the jar, stir, cover and leave it to ferment.

Day 14: Your mature starter will be elastic and appear bubbly whenever it is ready to use.

Store your sourdough discard in an airtight container. It will not need to be fed and it is ready to use straight from the fridge!

Starting on day 12, place a rubber band around the jar to mark the level of your starter right after it has been freshly fed. Set a timer for 4 to 6 hours and check on your starter. It should appear active and bubbly and should have doubled or tripled in volume, rising above the level of your rubber band. By day 14, it should rise predictably. (If it doesn't, your starter is not yet active and is unusable. Keep feeding it until it appears bubbly. If it grows mold, toss it and start over.)

Starting on day 10, rather than throwing away the portion of the starter you are not feeding, you can begin baking with this sourdough discard or store it indefinitely in a covered container in the refrigerator. This discard does not have to be refreshed, as it has enough acidity to prevent the growth of mold and harmful bacteria. Storing it in a cool place will slow down its activity and prevent it from becoming overly acidic. You'll be able to use this sourdough discard in many recipes in this book, including some of my favorites: Semolina Egg Pasta (page 93), Streusel Coffee Cake (page 134) and White Chocolate–Cranberry Oatmeal Cookies (page 148). However, this sourdough discard is not strong enough to leaven bread, so it is important to use active starter in the bread recipes.

MAINTAINING YOUR STARTER

Starting on day 14, your starter should have matured and be ready to use. At this point, you're no longer nurturing your starter to build strength; you're simply maintaining its activity so you can rely on it to make bread.

To maintain it, I recommend continuing as you did for days 10 to 14: Discard all but 14 grams (about 1 tablespoon) of starter and stir in 30 grams (¼ cup) of flour and 30 grams (2 tablespoons) of water. Feed it twice a day—except on days you are using it to bake. The yeast in the starter feeds on the starch in the flour in order to survive; once it digests all the available starch, it will starve. That means you have to replenish its food source. I've found that feeding my starter less often makes it sluggish and unpredictable, so I try to keep it on a regular feeding schedule.

As you get used to maintaining your starter, you'll find that you don't have to be strict about this process. Some people feed their starter just once a day and that works for their yeast. Choose a time of day that works best for your schedule, and as long as you are feeding your starter consistently (once or twice a day), it will stay healthy and active.

What if I forget to feed my starter? If you forget to feed your starter for a day or two, don't worry! It should be just fine. Feed it as soon as you remember, and then continue to follow your regular feeding schedule. You may notice a gray liquid starting to pool on top of your starter. This is called hooch; it's an alcoholic byproduct of the fermentation process. Hooch is completely safe, and you can either stir it into your starter or pour it out. Stirring in the hooch will give your starter a more acidic quality and can increase its sour flavor. Don't make a habit of neglecting your starter for long periods of time, though, as it may make your wild yeast too sluggish and even too weak to fight off mold and harmful bacteria. If you can't keep up with twice daily feedings, it's best to refrigerate your starter.

Can I refrigerate my starter? If your schedule does not permit you to maintain a once or twice daily feeding schedule, you can keep your starter in the refrigerator. Being in a cold environment weakens the yeast and slows down the rate at which they feed on the available flour, so you'll only need to feed your starter once a week. I only do this when I absolutely have to—when I go on vacation, for example—because I find that it weakens my starter and makes it unpredictable. However, if this is your sole option, take your starter out of the refrigerator two days before you want to make a loaf of bread and feed it two or three times a day. This will boost its activity and increase your chances of success.

UNDERSTANDING HOW TO USE YOUR SOURDOUGH STARTER

Active sourdough starter is a starter that has been freshly fed, looks bubbly and is strong enough to make bread rise. When you are using your sourdough starter to leaven bread, it's best to use it at its peak of activity, around 4 to 6 hours after it has been fed. Familiarize yourself with the signs of activity: an increase in volume (about double or triple the size before feeding) and an even distribution of bubbles throughout.

ACTIVE SOURDOUGH STARTER

Most of the bread recipes in this book simply call for you to use active sourdough starter at 100 percent hydration. This means your starter has been fed 4 to 6 hours before you start the recipe with an equal proportion of flour and water, by weight. For recipes that require a different level of hydration, I will specify right in the recipe the amount of flour and water that the starter needs.

In recipes that call for active sourdough starter, you'll need to plan ahead and make it yourself, using a ratio of one part sourdough starter to two parts flour and water. For example, for a bread recipe that calls for 113 grams (½ cup) of active sourdough starter, you'll need:

28 g (2 tbsp) sourdough starter

56 g (¼ cup) water

56 g (½ cup) all-purpose flour

Stir the ingredients together in a mixing bowl until they are fully combined. Set the bowl aside for 4 to 6 hours, or until your starter has at least doubled in volume, with an even distribution of bubbles throughout. This will make more than you need for your bread recipe. Measure out 113 grams (½ cup) for your recipe. Don't forget to keep back a small portion of starter (at least 14 grams [1 tablespoon]) in your starter jar and feed it with 30 grams (¼ cup) of flour and 30 grams (2 tablespoons) of water so you can perpetuate your starter.

There are many recipes in this book that use sourdough discard. This is the portion of your starter that you remove during feeding and that is not strong enough for breadmaking. Each time I discard some starter and feed the rest, I put that discard portion in a container that I keep in my refrigerator indefinitely.

Sourdough discard does not need to be fed, will keep just fine at cool temperatures and is always ready to use straight from the refrigerator. It is still able to ferment but is not robust enough to leaven bread. If you don't have a stockpile of it in your fridge, simply use some of your sourdough starter in the recipe instead.

Sourdough discard develops a very unique flavor as it continues to ferment. Using it as an ingredient in your baked goods can transform the flavor; it is not overpowering but adds complexity that manifests itself in a variety of ways. Unless your sourdough starter is excessively acidic, the results will not be overly sour. As you start adding sourdough discard to your baked goods, you'll begin to detect the signature flavor that is unique to sourdough.

KEYS TO BAKING GREAT BREAD

Understand bread, understand baking. —Paul Hollywood

Sourdough is alive, so it responds to its environment. Changes in the temperature, the humidity or the flour can have a marked effect on your baked goods. Recipes are great for exercising your creativity and trying new flavors, but they are not a magic formula. The key to good bread is to do your best to control the variables that affect what you bake—and if you can't, to understand the ways you can respond and adjust to get the best results.

Everything starts with your sourdough starter. The health and strength of your starter will always dictate the success of your bread. Care for your starter by feeding it regularly and keeping it at a constant temperature as much as possible. Remember, it's best to use your starter at the peak of activity—around 4 to 6 hours after it has been fed.

FLOUR

Flour makes up the bulk of your bread and is therefore the most important ingredient. Today, great quality flour is easy to find. Quality is important, so whenever possible I encourage you to buy organic flour from producers who care about how their product is harvested and processed. However, if it is not within your budget to do so, know that you can still create beautiful bread from non-organic flour. The most important thing is using the right *type* of flour. You can't easily substitute rye flour for whole wheat flour or all-purpose for bread flour. Doing so would affect the texture and quality of your bread. I specify the type of flour that will work best for each recipe in this book.

WEIGH YOUR INGREDIENTS

Although I provide volume measurements throughout this book, it's best to weigh your ingredients to achieve the most consistent results. That's why weight in grams is the first measurement for every ingredient in these recipes. I highly recommend buying a small digital kitchen scale (they're not expensive) and weighing your ingredients. Volume measurements are very inaccurate and you could actually double the flour called for in a recipe, depending on how you pack a measuring cup. To ensure the best possible outcome and consistent results, weigh everything. The best part? You won't have to wash multiple measuring cups.

TEMPERATURE

Ask any baker and they'll tell you that the most important ingredient in baking is temperature. It will make or break your bread. Temperature dictates the activity of the yeast and the rate of fermentation. Too cold and you'll end up with sluggish yeast that will drastically slow down the fermentation of your dough, so it will not rise properly. Too hot and your yeast will be overactive, difficult to control and could result in a flat, over-proofed loaf.

The ideal temperature for fermentation is between 76° and 78°F (24° and 25°C). I highly recommend purchasing an instant-read thermometer to help you measure the temperature of your dough throughout the breadmaking process.

These recipes are a guide; conditions in every kitchen are different, so adjust your process accordingly. In the summer when your kitchen is too hot, try adding cold water to your dough. If you find your kitchen is too cold, try proofing your dough in the oven with the light (not the heat!) turned on.

WATCH THE DOUGH, NOT THE CLOCK

The recipes and time estimates in this book account for fermenting and proofing in an environment that maintains a constant temperature of 78°F (25°C). If you cannot re-create these ideal conditions, you'll need to adjust the times: shorter fermentation and proofing periods for warmer temperatures and longer for colder ones. For example, if your kitchen is 85°F (29°C) one day, you may have to shorten your bulk fermentation period to 1 hour instead of the 2 hours specified in the recipe.

Instead of checking the time, watch for signs of fermentation. Bubbles, an increase in volume of 30 to 50 percent and a webby structure are usually good indications that the dough has adequately fermented and is ready to be shaped.

DON'T BE AFRAID TO GET YOUR HANDS DIRTY

I am an advocate of hand-mixing doughs. Your hands are the most important tools in your kitchen. For me, there is nothing quite like an afternoon spent with my hands buried in a bowl of dough. By using your hands, you'll be able to learn what dough is supposed to feel like at each step of the breadmaking process, when the dough is strong enough and when it hasn't fermented enough. At first it may feel gross to get your hands caked in dough, but you'll soon find ways of handling delicate doughs. If your dough is too sticky, wet your hands when you fold it during the kneading process.

YOUR FIRST LOAF

Congratulations! Your starter has matured and you're ready to bake your first loaf of bread. As you've learned by now, there are a lot of nuances in baking sourdough. In this chapter, I'll go into detail about each of the steps involved in creating your dough and baking a loaf, including how to activate your starter. It may seem complicated at first, but with practice, this process will begin to feel like second nature. Throughout the recipes in this book, I will refer to the techniques I detail in this chapter, so it's important to familiarize yourself with them.

BEGINNER'S SOURDOUGH BREAD

This recipe is simple to follow and easy to handle because of its low water content, making it a great recipe for anyone who is new to baking with sourdough. You may not end up with larger holes in your bread the first time you try this recipe, but if you follow the tips here, you'll end up with a delicious loaf with a nice, even and tender crumb.

ACTIVE SOURDOUGH STARTER

23 g (1½ tbsp) sourdough starter

45 g (¼ cup) water

45 g (½ cup) bread flour

DOUGH

226 g (1 cup) water

339 g (2¾ cups) bread flour

120 g (½ cup) active sourdough starter

9 g (1½ tsp) salt

TOOLS YOU'LL NEED

2 large mixing bowls

Kitchen scale

Banneton or medium mixing bowl

Clean kitchen towel

A little rice flour

Dutch oven or bread cloche (5 quarts [4.7 L] or larger)

Parchment paper

Lame or sharp knife

NOTE: A few of the tools listed here may be unfamiliar. A *banneton* is a type of basket, usually made of rattan, that is used to provide structure for shaped loaves during proofing. A *bread cloche* is a baking pan with a tight-fitting dome that helps trap steam as the bread bakes. A *lame* is a sharp slashing tool made just for scoring bread.

DAY 1

ACTIVATE YOUR SOURDOUGH STARTER

Combine the sourdough starter, water and bread flour in a small bowl. Cover the bowl with plastic wrap and set it aside in a warm place until your starter appears noticeably bubbly and has doubled in volume. This activates your starter, allowing it to build up enough yeast and enough strength to leaven bread. Your starter will be at its most active 4 to 6 hours after it has been fed. Remember to keep a portion of your starter back to maintain and feed.

AUTOLYZE

Three hours after you feed your starter, mix the water and bread flour for the dough in a large mixing bowl. Cover the bowl with plastic wrap and set it aside to rest for about 1 hour while your starter continues to activate.

Autolyze is a very complicated-sounding word for an extremely simple process. It just means mixing flour and water and allowing it to rest before incorporating any other ingredients. When the water is absorbed by the flour, it activates enzymes, gluten development begins and simple sugars start to form as starch is broken down. It may look as if nothing is happening, but this process helps develop strength in your dough. After the autolyze, your dough will appear noticeably smooth and will be much less sticky and easier to handle.

(Continued)

STRETCH AND FOLD

Grab a portion of the dough and stretch it toward you.

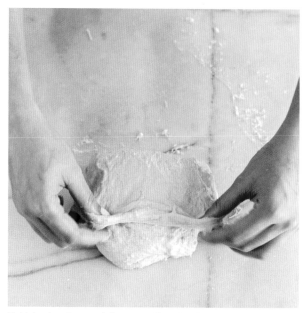

Fold the dough toward the center. Turn the dough and repeat this process until all sides have been folded.

BULK FERMENTATION

Add the active sourdough starter, along with the salt, to the autolyzed dough. Let the mixture rest for 30 minutes. This marks the beginning of **bulk fermentation**.

> **Bulk fermentation** is a vital part of breadmaking. It begins when activated sourdough starter is added to the rest of the dough ingredients. During this stage, the dough ferments in one mass before it is divided or shaped into a loaf (or loaves). The success of your bread depends largely on bulk fermentation. This is when the structure of your bread develops and when your yeast produces the carbon dioxide that gives your dough volume and lightness. Depending on the temperature of your kitchen, the total time for bulk fermentation could be anywhere from 4 to 6 hours. Use a timer to keep track of the time between stretch and folds and to remind you when bulk fermentation should be complete.

After about 30 minutes, it's time to **stretch and fold**.

> **Stretch and folds** create strength and organize the gluten network in your dough. A strong gluten network allows your dough to trap carbon dioxide so your bread can rise.

Start by picking up one side of the dough with both of your hands and stretching it as far as you can.

Fold it over itself, turn the bowl 90 degrees and repeat until all sides of the dough have been folded. This is one set.

Perform four to six sets of stretch and folds, 30 minutes apart, until the dough feels strong and has passed the **windowpane test**. Depending on the temperature of your kitchen, this step of the process could take 4 to 6 hours.

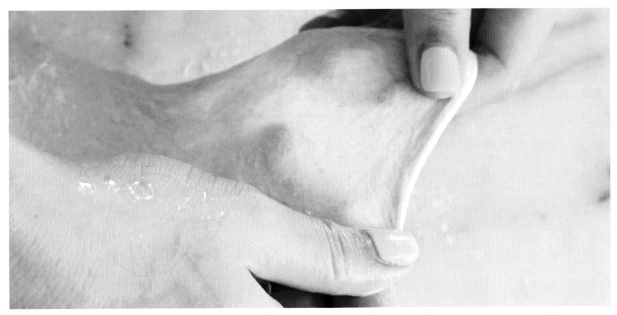

Once you've reached the windowpane stage, your dough will feel elastic, appear translucent and will not tear when gently stretched.

The **windowpane test** is one of the best ways to tell whether you've successfully built up enough gluten in your dough. Gently spread the dough using your fingers. If you can stretch the dough out into a thin membrane that you can see through without breaking it, your dough has passed the windowpane test.

After you've completed your last set of stretch and folds and your dough has passed the windowpane test, cover the bowl with plastic wrap and allow it to ferment undisturbed in a warm spot for 1 to 3 hours. At the end of bulk fermentation, your dough should have increased in volume by 30 to 50 percent, and feel airy, and the surface should appear smooth with a webby structure and lots of bubbles throughout.

While other bread recipes may call for your dough to double in size, when it comes to making crusty rustic breads, the yeast has usually exhausted all its food supply by the time your dough doubles in volume. To avoid over-proofing your dough, end bulk fermentation when your dough appears bubbly, has a webby structure and has increased in volume by 30 to 50 percent. Remember, fermentation is greatly dependent on temperature, so if your dough has not risen, move it to a warmer spot in your kitchen and continue with bulk fermentation.

(Continued)

BOULE

1

Gently coax the dough from the bowl onto a lightly floured work surface and use your fingers to spread it out slightly.

2

Fold the bottom part of the dough toward the middle.

3

Gently stretch the right and left sides and fold each toward the middle.

4

Fold the top portion of the dough toward the middle and flip your dough over.

5

Rotate the dough on the counter to create surface tension.

6

Place the shaped boule seam-side up into a banneton with a cloth liner dusted with rice flour or a mixing bowl lined with a kitchen towel dusted with rice flour.

SHAPING

As you shape your dough into a boule or batard, be very gentle to avoid knocking air out of your loaf. Handling your dough gently will help you have larger holes throughout your loaf, making it more airy. The goal when shaping is to create an appropriate amount of tension in your dough; the surface should look smooth and tight. This will encourage a good rise when it's in your oven.

BATARD

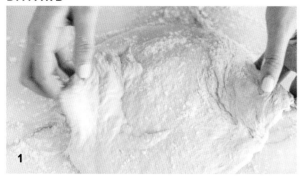

1

Gently coax the dough from the bowl onto a lightly floured work surface and use your fingers to spread it out slightly.

2

Gently stretch the right and left sides and fold each toward the middle.

3

Roll your dough starting with the side away from you.

4

Flip your dough over.

5

Drag the dough lightly on the counter to create surface tension.

6

Place the shaped batard seam-side up into a banneton with a cloth liner dusted with rice flour.

Take advantage of the tools you already have in your kitchen. If you don't have a banneton, a small mixing bowl lined with a kitchen towel works perfectly. Just don't forget to dust the kitchen towel liberally with rice flour to prevent the dough from sticking. If you don't have a lame, use a sharp paring knife to score your dough.

(Continued)

Wrap your shaped dough in a plastic bag to prevent it from drying out while it proofs in the refrigerator

PROOFING

Carefully place your shaped loaf in a banneton or a mixing bowl as previously instructed. Place in a plastic bag (a clean shopping bag works well here) and seal it, to keep the dough from drying out. Then place it in your refrigerator for a final **proof** overnight.

If you're using your banneton for the first time, you'll need to season it first. Lightly spray it with tap water and dust it liberally with all-purpose flour. Tip out any excess. You can skip the seasoning step if you will be using your banneton with a cloth liner. Just remember to dust the liner with rice flour to prevent your dough from sticking. I recommend rice flour because it contains no gluten, so the dough won't stick to the flour and therefore can't get stuck to the banneton.

Proofing is the final rise after the dough has been shaped into a loaf and before it is baked. A long, cold proof in the refrigerator slows down the natural yeast, allowing your dough to develop more flavor while preventing it from becoming over-proofed.

Hold your lame at a 30- to 45-degree angle to the dough surface to promote the formation of a small flap, known as an ear. The cut should only be ¼ inch to ½ inch (0.6 to 1.27 cm) deep.

DAY 2

When you're ready to bake, put your Dutch oven in the oven and preheat it to 500°F (260°C). When your oven is at the right temperature, gently turn the dough out onto a piece of parchment paper. Using a sharp knife, or a lame if you have one, make a long, shallow slash (about ¼ inch [5 mm] deep) across the top of your loaf. Once you're more comfortable with the breadmaking process, you may choose to **score** your loaf with decorative patterns.

Scoring, or cutting your loaf, creates a weak point in the dough where steam can escape and bread can expand in a controlled manner during baking. Skipping this step will result in blowouts in your loaf.

Gently transfer the dough, with the parchment paper, into your hot Dutch oven. Bake your loaf covered for 30 minutes and then uncovered for 10 to 15 minutes, depending on how dark you'd like your crust.

Steam keeps the crust soft during the first minutes of baking so the loaf can continue to rise and achieve a final expansion. Professional bread ovens are fitted with steam injectors; the easiest way to mimic this in your home kitchen is by baking in a Dutch oven or a bread cloche. Water that evaporates during baking becomes trapped inside the pan, dissolving sugars on the surface of the dough that caramelize during baking and give the bread a shiny, crispy crust.

Place your finished loaf on a wire rack and allow it to cool for at least 2 hours before slicing. Once you smell the aroma of your fresh-baked bread, it may be tempting to cut into it immediately. However, slicing your loaf too soon will result in an undesirable gummy crumb that could cause your bread to dry out and go stale more quickly.

Store leftover bread in a paper bag in more humid climates or in a plastic bag in drier environments.

CRUSTY RUSTIC BREADS

A great sourdough loaf has a hearty crust encasing a soft, silky crumb. You'll use the steps and skills you learned in the first two chapters to successfully make all of the breads in this one. These recipes showcase the versatility of sourdough, and you'll see how simple substitutions and additions can radically change both the flavor profile and the texture of bread. Cornmeal and corn flour impart a rich flavor and soft crumb to the Buttered Polenta Loaf (page 32), and a warm mix of spice and chocolate transforms sourdough into a brownie-like dessert bread in the Mexican Hot Chocolate Rye Loaf (page 39).

WHOLE WHEAT COUNTRY LOAF

The high proportion of whole wheat flour gives this loaf a deliciously nutty flavor and a heartier texture. The bran in whole wheat flour can interfere with gluten development and inhibit dough from rising, but soaking it overnight helps ensure a taller rise and an airy crumb.

MAKES 1 LOAF

SOAKER

150 g (1¼ cups) whole wheat flour

150 g (⅔ cup) warm water

DOUGH

180 g (1½ cups) bread flour

150 g (⅔ cup) warm water

75 g (⅓ cup) active sourdough starter (see page 15)

6 g (1 tsp) salt

THE NIGHT BEFORE

Make your **soaker** by combining the whole wheat flour and water in an airtight container. Place it in the refrigerator overnight.

> A **soaker** is dough made with whole wheat flour and water, mixed a few hours or even days before being added to the rest of the recipe ingredients. Mixing whole wheat flour with water in advance softens the sharp edges of the bran and prevents it from interfering with gluten development.

DAY 1

First thing in the morning, take your soaker out of the refrigerator to allow it to warm up to room temperature.

To make the dough, in a large bowl combine the bread flour and water. Mix until all the flour is hydrated.

Cover the bowl with plastic wrap and allow the dough to autolyze for at least an hour.

Fold your activated starter, the soaker and the salt into your autolyzed dough until the mixture sticks together and forms a homogenous dough. Cover the bowl with plastic wrap and set aside for 30 minutes.

During bulk fermentation, perform four to six stretch and folds at 30-minute intervals. Continue the stretch and folds until your dough has passed the windowpane test (page 23). After your last fold, allow the dough to rest untouched in the covered bowl for 1½ to 3 hours, depending on the temperature of your kitchen. At the end of bulk fermentation, your dough should look bubbly and should have risen by 30 to 50 percent.

After bulk fermentation, turn your dough out onto a lightly floured work surface, round it gently, cover it with plastic wrap and allow it to rest on your countertop for 30 minutes.

Shape the dough into a boule or batard (see pages 24–25) and gently put it into your prepared banneton or lined mixing bowl. Put the banneton in a plastic bag to prevent it from drying out, and place the dough in the refrigerator overnight.

DAY 2

Place your Dutch oven in the oven and preheat it to 500°F (260°C). Score your loaf and carefully place it in the hot Dutch oven. Bake covered for 30 minutes and uncovered for 10 to 15 minutes.

Place your loaf on a wire rack to cool for at least 2 hours before slicing. Store in a paper bag in more humid climates or in a plastic bag in drier environments.

BUTTERED POLENTA LOAF

The addition of corn flour and cornmeal imparts an incredibly rich flavor to this loaf. Polenta holds a lot of moisture, which makes this dough wet and may make it more difficult to handle. But it's worth the effort, because this added moisture helps give the crumb a much softer texture.

MAKES 1 LOAF

POLENTA

14 g (1 tbsp) unsalted butter

20 g (1½ tbsp) yellow cornmeal

226 g (1 cup) water

DOUGH

75 g (⅓ cup) active sourdough starter (see page 15)

226 g (1 cup) water

300 g (2½ cups) bread flour

60 g (¼ cup) corn flour

6 g (1 tsp) salt

DAY 1

To make the polenta, melt the butter in a small saucepan over medium heat. When it has melted, add the cornmeal and sauté for 1 minute. Then add the water, stirring constantly to prevent the polenta from burning. Cook until the mixture has thickened, about 3 to 5 minutes. Set aside and cool completely.

To make the dough, in a large mixing bowl combine the active starter, water, bread flour, corn flour and salt. Stir with a wooden spoon or your hand until all the ingredients have been incorporated. Resist the urge to add more water to the dough; the polenta will release a lot of moisture once it's been added. Cover the bowl with plastic wrap and set aside for 1 hour.

After the rest period, gradually fold the polenta into the dough. Your dough should look cohesive, with specs of polenta distributed throughout. It will feel wet but solid and shouldn't feel like it will fall apart. Cover the bowl with plastic wrap and set aside for 30 minutes.

Throughout bulk fermentation, perform four to six stretch and folds at 30-minute intervals. Continue folding until your dough has passed the windowpane test (page 23). After your last fold, cover the bowl with plastic wrap and leave the dough to rest untouched for 1½ to 3 hours, depending on the temperature of your kitchen. At the end of bulk fermentation, your dough should look bubbly and should have risen by 30 to 50 percent.

After bulk fermentation, turn the dough out on a lightly floured work surface, gently round it, cover with plastic wrap and leave it to rest on your countertop for 30 minutes.

Shape the dough into a boule or batard (see pages 24–25) and gently put it into your prepared banneton or lined mixing bowl. Wrap the banneton in a plastic bag to prevent it from drying out before placing it in the refrigerator overnight.

DAY 2

Put your Dutch oven in the oven and preheat it to 500°F (260°C). Score your loaf and gently place it in the hot Dutch oven. Bake covered for 30 minutes and uncovered for 10 to 15 minutes.

Place your loaf on a wire rack and allow it to cool for at least 2 hours before slicing. Store leftover bread in a paper bag in more humid climates or in a plastic bag in drier environments.

SEMOLINA CHILI-CHEDDAR LOAF

Floral notes and the mild spice of Fresno chilies are a perfect complement to the tanginess of sourdough. Substitute different types of chilies depending on your love or tolerance for heat. Use bell peppers for those with a delicate palate or serranos for spice lovers.

MAKES 1 LOAF

280 g (2⅓ cups) bread flour

80 g (⅔ cup) fine semolina flour

282 g (1¼ cups) warm water

75 g (⅓ cup) active sourdough starter (see page 15)

7 g (1 tsp) salt

58 g (½ cup) thinly sliced cheddar cheese

22 g (¼ cup) sliced Fresno chilies

DAY 1

In a large mixing bowl, combine the bread flour, semolina flour and water. Mix until all the flour is hydrated. Cover the bowl with plastic wrap and allow dough to autolyze for 1 hour.

In another large mixing bowl, combine the autolyzed dough, active starter and salt. Keep folding until the mixture forms a cohesive, homogenous dough. Cover the bowl with plastic wrap and set aside for 30 minutes.

Wet your countertop slightly, turn your dough out and flatten it into a rectangle. Spread the cheese and peppers evenly over the top. Use your hands to roll the dough into a log, flatten it slightly and fold the ends toward the middle. Return the stuffed dough to the bowl. Cover with plastic wrap and set aside for 30 minutes.

During bulk fermentation, perform four to six stretch and folds at 30-minute intervals. Continue folding until your dough has passed the windowpane test (page 23). After your last fold, allow the dough to rest untouched in the covered bowl for 1½ to 3 hours, depending on the temperature of your kitchen. At the end of bulk fermentation, your dough should look bubbly and should have risen by 30 to 50 percent.

After bulk fermentation, turn your dough out onto a lightly floured surface, round it gently, cover with plastic wrap and allow it to rest on your countertop for 30 minutes.

Shape the dough into a boule or batard (see pages 24–25) and gently put it into your prepared banneton or lined mixing bowl. Wrap the banneton in a plastic bag to prevent it from drying out before placing it in the refrigerator overnight.

DAY 2

Put your Dutch oven in the oven and preheat it to 500°F (260°C). Score your loaf and gently place it in the hot Dutch oven. Bake covered for 30 minutes and uncovered for 10 to 15 minutes.

Place the loaf on a wire rack and allow it to cool for at least 2 hours before slicing. Store leftover bread in a paper bag in more humid climates or in a plastic bag in drier environments.

CHAI-SPICED GOJI BERRY SPELT LOAF

Infused with chai tea, this loaf features the bold flavors of cardamom, cinnamon and cloves. Fresh pops of goji berry throughout make this bread really unique and delicious. Honey increases the activity of the wild yeast and complements the natural sweetness of the spelt flour—made from a type of wheat that has been cultivated since the Bronze Age.

MAKES 1 LOAF

226 g (1 cup) hot water

1 bag (1 tsp loose leaf) chai tea

30 g (⅓ cup) goji berries

240 g (2 cups) bread flour

60 g (½ cup) spelt flour

4 g (½ tsp) kosher salt

16 g (1 tbsp) honey

113 g (½ cup) active sourdough starter (see page 15)

DAY 1

Pour the hot water into a small bowl and add the tea and goji berries. Steep for 10 minutes. Dispose of the tea bag, then strain out the goji berries and set aside. Cool the tea to room temperature.

In a large bowl, combine the bread flour, spelt flour and salt. Add the tea, honey and active starter. Stir and fold until it forms a cohesive dough. Cover the bowl with plastic wrap and set aside for 30 minutes.

Wet your countertop slightly, then turn the dough out and flatten it into a rectangle. Distribute the goji berries evenly on top of the dough and use your hands to roll it into a log. Flatten the log slightly, fold the ends toward the middle and return the dough to the bowl. Cover with plastic wrap and set aside for 30 minutes.

During bulk fermentation, perform four to six stretch and folds at 30-minute intervals. Continue folding until your dough has passed the windowpane test (page 23). After your last fold, allow the dough to rest untouched in the covered bowl for 1½ to 3 hours, depending on the temperature of your kitchen. At the end of bulk fermentation, your dough should look bubbly and should have risen by 30 to 50 percent.

After bulk fermentation, turn your dough out onto a lightly floured work surface, round it gently, cover it with plastic wrap and allow it to rest on your countertop for 30 minutes.

Shape the dough into a boule or batard (see pages 24–25) and gently put it into your prepared banneton or lined mixing bowl. Wrap the banneton in a plastic bag to prevent it from drying out before placing it in the refrigerator overnight.

DAY 2

Put your Dutch oven in the oven and preheat it to 500°F (260°C). Score your loaf and gently place it in the hot Dutch oven. Bake covered for 30 minutes and uncovered for 10 to 15 minutes.

Place the loaf on a wire rack and allow it to cool for at least 2 hours before slicing. Store leftover bread in a paper bag in more humid climates or in a plastic bag in drier environments.

MEXICAN HOT CHOCOLATE RYE LOAF

This loaf is inspired by one of my favorite places, Oaxaca, Mexico, where cacao is considered sacred and hot chocolate is a daily staple. Oaxacan hot chocolate celebrates the bitter complexity of cocoa, tempered by sweet raw sugar and warm cinnamon. The addition of rye adds a slight earthiness and accentuates the tanginess of the sourdough. Baking this loaf will fill your kitchen with the delicious smell of chocolate, and though it may be tempting to cut into it as soon as you pull it out of the oven, your patience will pay off as the crumb sets and flavors meld while the loaf cools.

MAKES 1 LOAF

300 g (2½ cups) bread flour

30 g (¼ cup) rye flour

15 g (2 tbsp) Dutch-process cocoa powder

4 g (1 tsp) ground cinnamon

¼ tsp cayenne pepper (optional)

2 g (1 tsp) ground nutmeg

6 g (1 tsp) kosher salt

28 g (2 tbsp) brown sugar

113 g (½ cup) active sourdough starter (see page 15)

226 g (1 cup) warm water

DAY 1

In a large mixing bowl, whisk together the bread flour, rye flour, cocoa powder, cinnamon, cayenne pepper (if using), nutmeg and salt until no lumps remain. Add the brown sugar, active starter and water. Stir the ingredients together and fold until it forms a cohesive, homogenous dough. Cover the bowl with plastic wrap and set aside for 30 minutes.

During bulk fermentation, perform four to six stretch and folds at 30-minute intervals. Continue folding until your dough has passed the windowpane test (page 23). After your last fold, allow the dough to rest untouched in the covered bowl for 1½ to 3 hours, depending on the temperature of your kitchen. At the end of bulk fermentation, your dough should look bubbly and should have risen by 30 to 50 percent.

After bulk fermentation, turn your dough out onto a lightly floured work surface, round your dough gently, cover it with plastic wrap and allow it to rest on your countertop for 30 minutes.

Shape the dough into a boule or batard (see pages 24–25) and gently put it into your prepared banneton or lined mixing bowl. Wrap the banneton in a plastic bag to prevent it from drying out before placing it in the refrigerator overnight.

DAY 2

Put your Dutch oven in the oven and preheat it to 500°F (260°C). Score your loaf and gently place it in the hot Dutch oven. Bake covered for 30 minutes and uncovered for 10 to 15 minutes.

Place the loaf on a wire rack and allow it to cool for at least 2 hours before slicing. Store leftover bread in a paper bag in more humid climates or in a plastic bag in drier environments.

SOFT SANDWICH LOAVES AND FLUFFY ROLLS

Soft sandwich loaves and rolls were probably the first types of bread I ever ate—although the ones I had were always made with ingredients I couldn't pronounce and came in a plastic bag. It's no wonder it was so easy for me to swear off bread before I discovered sourdough. Using sourdough to leaven dough enriched with milk, butter and other dairy products allows you to take advantage of the magic of fermentation, which makes these breads much easier to digest. From the Cracked Barley Sandwich Loaf (page 43) to Honey Butter Rolls (page 55), these recipes put a healthier spin on the classics.

CRACKED BARLEY SANDWICH LOAF

Cracked barley is barley that has been hulled and then put through a cracker to break the kernels into pieces. This is my version of the classic whole wheat sandwich loaf. This hearty bread has a nutty flavor, and thanks to an extended fermentation, you'll be able to take advantage of all the nutrients in barley and whole wheat. Baking with steam for the first few minutes prevents the crust from hardening and allows your loaf to have one final burst of expansion in the oven. I bake this loaf in a Pullman pan, a narrow loaf pan with straight sides. If you don't have one, a regular loaf pan will work just fine.

MAKES 1 LOAF

SOAKER

45 g (¼ cup) cracked barley

Boiling water

240 g (2 cups) whole wheat flour

226 g (1 cup) whole milk

DOUGH

120 g (1 cup) bread flour

80 g (⅓ cup) warm water

75 g (⅓ cup) active sourdough starter (see page 15)

6 g (1 tsp) salt

28 g (2 tbsp) honey

42 g (3 tbsp) unsalted butter, softened

17 g (1 tbsp) vegetable oil

THE NIGHT BEFORE

To make the soaker, in a small bowl, soak the cracked barley for 30 minutes in enough boiling water to cover it, then drain. Combine the whole wheat flour, milk and drained barley in a medium bowl and stir until everything is fully incorporated. Store in an airtight container overnight in the refrigerator.

DAY 1

In a large bowl, combine the bread flour, water, active starter, salt and soaker. Stir the mixture with your hands or a spatula until it forms a cohesive dough. Turn the dough out onto a lightly floured work surface and knead it for 10 minutes. Return the dough to your bowl and stir in the honey, butter and oil until they are fully incorporated. On a lightly floured work surface, knead the dough for another 15 minutes. Return it to the bowl, cover the bowl with plastic wrap and set aside for 1 hour.

Your main goal in kneading is to fully incorporate the ingredients and create strength and elasticity in the dough. My favorite way to knead is to flatten and stretch the dough out, then fold it back on itself and repeat the process.

On a lightly floured work surface, knead the dough for another 10 to 15 minutes, until it passes the windowpane test (page 23). Return it to the bowl, cover the bowl with plastic wrap and allow it to rest on the countertop untouched for 2 to 3 hours, depending on the temperature of your kitchen. At the end of bulk fermentation, your dough should look bubbly and should have risen by 30 to 50 percent.

(Continued)

Turn the dough out onto a lightly floured work surface. Deflate it by pushing down on it, then flatten it into a 10-inch (25-cm) square. Fold the bottom up to the middle. Then fold each side toward the middle—your dough should look like an open envelope. Now grab the top edge and gently roll down so you have a long tube.

Transfer the shaped dough to a 9 x 4–inch (23 x 10–cm) Pullman pan. Wrap the pan in a plastic bag and let it proof in the refrigerator overnight.

DAY 2

When you're ready to bake, set a rack in the middle of the oven and a baking pan on the bottom rack. Preheat your oven to 500°F (260°C). Bring 2 cups (480 ml) of water to a boil. Pour 1 cup (240 ml) of water into the baking pan, close the door and allow steam to build up in the oven.

Take your loaf out of the refrigerator and score the top. Place your loaf in the oven and quickly pour the remaining water into the baking pan. Bake the loaf for 20 minutes with steam, then remove the baking pan from the oven and bake the loaf for another 30 minutes without steam.

Place your loaf on a wire rack and allow it to cool for at least 4 hours or overnight before slicing. (If you cut your loaf too soon, it will be very gummy due to the high percentage of whole wheat.) Store the bread in a ziptop bag at room temperature for up to 1 week.

*See photo on page 42.

ORANGE-CRANBERRY MILK BREAD

Milk bread is pillowy soft and stays tender for days after baking. Thanks to the **tangzhong** technique, this bread holds more moisture and will remain fresh for longer. Orange and cranberry are the perfect complement to this cloudlike loaf that's best enjoyed without any toppings at all.

Tangzhong is a technique that originated in Asia for making soft, fluffy yeast bread. It involves cooking a small portion of the flour and liquid into a thick slurry before adding the remaining ingredients. This slurry locks moisture into the dough and prevents it from drying out and getting stale too quickly.

MAKES 1 LOAF

TANGZHONG STARTER

15 g (2 tbsp) all-purpose flour

56 g (¼ cup) whole milk

56 g (¼ cup) water

DOUGH

322 g (2⅔ cups) bread flour

5 g (¾ tsp) kosher salt

42 g (3 tbsp) granulated sugar

Zest of 1 orange

75 g (⅓ cup) whole milk

1 large egg

113 g (½ cup) active sourdough starter (see page 15)

57 g (4 tbsp) unsalted butter, softened

60 g (½ cup) dried cranberries

EGG WASH

1 egg white

5 g (1 tsp) whole milk

Pinch of salt

DAY 1

To make the tangzhong starter, combine the flour, milk and water in a small saucepan over low heat and whisk until no lumps remain. Cook the mixture, stirring constantly, until it's slightly thickened, about 3 to 5 minutes. Remove from the heat and allow the tangzhong starter to cool completely.

To make the dough, in a large mixing bowl, whisk together the flour, salt, sugar and orange zest. Add the milk, cooled tangzhong starter, egg and active sourdough starter. Stir until the dough looks fully incorporated. Knead the dough on a lightly floured surface for about 5 minutes. Add the butter 14 grams (1 tablespoon) at a time, kneading after each addition. When the butter is fully incorporated, knead the dough for an additional 10 minutes.

Round the dough into a tight ball and place it in a lightly oiled bowl. Cover the bowl with plastic wrap and set it in a warm spot in your kitchen. After 1 hour, knead the dough again for about 5 minutes. Place the dough in a clean, lightly oiled bowl and cover it with plastic wrap.

(Continued)

Allow the dough to rise for 4 to 6 hours, or until it has increased in volume by 30 to 50 percent, looks bubbly and has a webby structure. Deflate the dough by pushing down on it, then shape it into a tight ball and place it inside an airtight container. Refrigerate overnight.

DAY 2

Turn the dough out onto a lightly floured work surface and divide it into four equal portions. Flatten each piece into a 3 x 6–inch (7.5 x 15–cm) rectangle and sprinkle one-quarter of the cranberries on top of each dough portion. Roll each into a tight log and nestle them side by side in a 8 x 4–inch (20 x 10–cm) loaf pan. Cover the pan with plastic wrap and set in a warm place. Allow the dough to proof for 2 to 4 hours, or until it looks puffy and resembles the texture of marshmallows.

Preheat the oven to 350°F (175°C).

To make the egg wash, in a small bowl, beat together the egg white, milk and salt. Brush the top of the loaf with the egg wash. Bake for 25 to 30 minutes, until the top is golden brown.

Remove the loaf from the oven. Allow it to cool in the pan for 10 minutes, then transfer it to a rack to cool completely. Store the cooled loaf at room temperature in a ziptop bag for 3 or 4 days.

POTATO SANDWICH LOAF

Potatoes hold more moisture than flour, which helps this sandwich loaf stay soft and fresh for days. Sourdough elevates the flavor and potatoes make this bread heartier than a conventional all-white sandwich loaf.

MAKES 1 LOAF

DOUGH

300 g (2½ cups) all-purpose flour

28 g (2 tbsp) granulated sugar

4 g (½ tsp) salt

113 g (½ cup) whole milk

113 g (½ cup) active sourdough starter (see page 15)

200 g (½ cup) cooked and mashed russet potato

28 g (2 tbsp) unsalted butter, softened

EGG WASH

1 egg white

7 g (1 tsp) water

Pinch of salt

DAY 1

In a large bowl, combine the flour, sugar and salt. Make a well in the middle and add the milk, active starter and mashed potato. Stir all the ingredients together with a spatula or your hand until the dough is fully mixed. On a lightly floured surface, knead the dough for about 5 minutes to develop strength and structure. Add the butter and then knead for an additional 10 minutes.

Return the dough to the bowl, cover with plastic wrap and allow the dough to rest for 1 hour. Turn it out onto a lightly floured surface, knead for 5 minutes and shape it into a ball. Lightly oil the bowl and place the dough in it, cover with plastic wrap and allow the dough to rise at room temperature until it's almost doubled in volume, 4 to 6 hours.

When the dough has doubled in volume and appears bubbly, deflate it by pressing down with your hands, round the dough into a tight ball and return it to the bowl. Cover with plastic wrap and refrigerate overnight.

DAY 2

Turn the dough out onto a lightly floured surface. Deflate it by pushing down on it, then flatten it into a 10-inch (25-cm) square. Fold the bottom up to the middle. Then fold each side toward the middle—your dough should look like an open envelope. Now grab the top edge and gently roll down into a long tube.

Transfer the shaped dough into a 9 x 4–inch (23 x 10–cm) Pullman pan. Wrap the pan in a plastic bag and leave it to proof for 2 to 4 hours, or until the dough has doubled in volume and appears puffy, with a marshmallowy texture.

Preheat the oven to 350°F (175°C).

To make the egg wash, in a small bowl, beat together the egg white, water and salt. Brush the top of the loaf with the egg wash.

Bake the loaf for 30 to 35 minutes, or until it's golden brown and the temperature registers 190°F (88°C) when probed with a thermometer.

Remove the loaf from the pan and cool it on a wire rack for 1 hour before slicing. Allow the loaf to cool completely and store it uncut in a ziptop bag for up to 1 week at room temperature.

BRAIDED BRIOCHE

Brioche is a classic French bread with a rich, tender crumb that's almost cake-like. This dough gets most of its moisture from eggs and butter, so you'll need to cut down the amount of liquid in your starter by creating a stiff active sourdough starter. The high proportion of dairy helps produce this loaf's fluffy crumb, but it also makes the dough very soft and difficult to handle—which is why it's easier to mix this dough in a stand mixer. Be patient and use a light hand while braiding.

MAKES 1 LOAF

STIFF ACTIVE SOURDOUGH STARTER

28 g (2 tbsp) sourdough starter

28 g (2 tbsp) warm water

90 g (¾ cup) all-purpose flour

DOUGH

360 g (3 cups) all-purpose flour

72 g (⅓ cup) granulated sugar

7 g (1 tsp) kosher salt

56 g (¼ cup) whole milk

4 large eggs

170 g (¾ cup) unsalted butter, chilled

EGG WASH

1 egg white

7 g (1 tsp) water

Pinch of salt

DAY 1

To make the stiff active sourdough starter, in a large container with an airtight lid, combine the sourdough starter, water and flour. Mix thoroughly. Set aside and allow your starter to activate for about 4 to 6 hours.

To make the dough, in the bowl of a stand mixer fitted with a dough hook, combine the flour, sugar, salt, active starter, milk and eggs, and mix and knead the ingredients together for 10 minutes. Using a stand mixer is the easiest way to get the best results with brioche, but if you don't have one, you can mix the dough by hand. This dough can feel quite wet, so if it feels too sticky, I suggest letting it rest for 30 minutes, then checking again. Knead the dough for 10 minutes, then let it rest for 30 minutes, repeating until the dough looks smooth and supple.

Place the butter between two large pieces of parchment paper and use a rolling pin to flatten and soften it. With the mixer running, add the butter to the dough a little bit at a time. When the butter is fully incorporated, continue mixing the dough until it sticks to the hook and makes a slapping noise against the sides of the bowl, 5 to 10 minutes.

Gather the dough into a tight ball and place it in a clean bowl. Cover the bowl with plastic wrap and allow it to rise untouched in a warm spot for 4 to 6 hours, or until it has doubled in volume. Deflate it by pushing down on it, then shape it into a tight ball, place it in an airtight container and refrigerate overnight.

DAY 2

Line a large sheet pan with parchment paper.

Turn the dough out onto a lightly floured work surface. Knock the air out and divide the dough into six equal portions. Use your hands to roll out each piece into a rope about 16 inches (40 cm) long. Line the pieces up vertically and pinch them together at the top. Fan them out from that central point at the top.

(Continued)

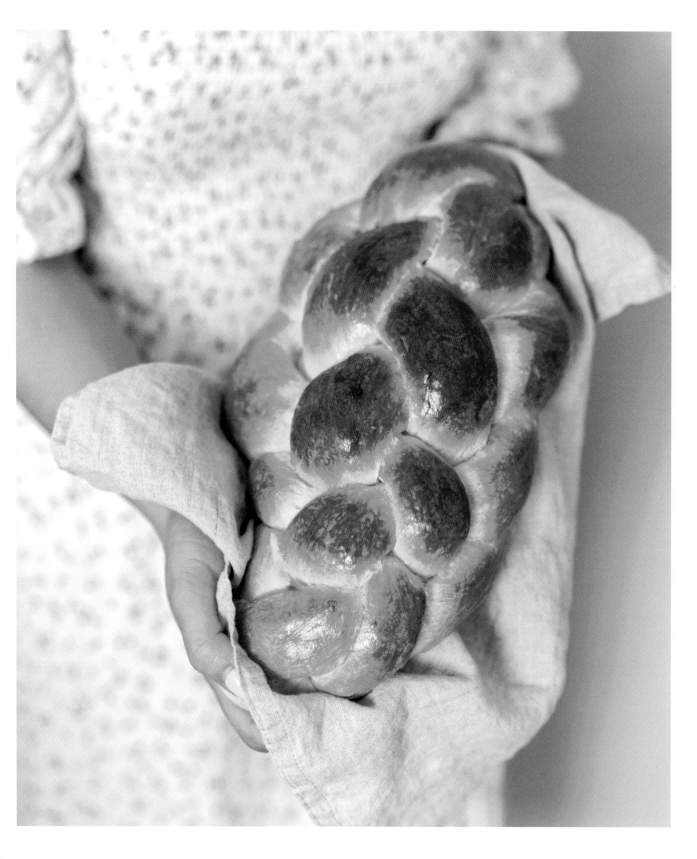

Number the strands of dough from 1 to 6, from left to right. Every time you move a strand, it will take the number of its position in the line. (For example, moving strand 6 to position 1 will make that strand the new 1.) Please see the photo series below for step-by-step braiding instructions.

Place the loaf on the lined sheet pan. Cover the loaf with lightly oiled plastic wrap and leave it to proof for 2 to 4 hours, or until the dough has doubled in volume and resembles the texture of marshmallows.

Preheat the oven to 350°F (175°C).

To make the egg wash, in a small bowl, beat together the egg white, water and salt. Brush the top of the loaf with the egg wash. Bake for 35 to 40 minutes, until the outside is golden brown.

Remove the loaf from the pan and transfer it to a rack to cool completely. Store at room temperature in a ziptop bag for up to 1 week.

TO BRAID THE LOAF:

Lay out the strands and fan them from a central point at the top. Going from left to right, number them from 1 to 6.

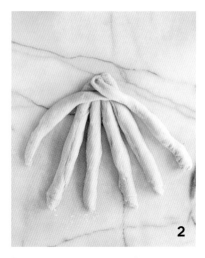

Pick up strands 6 and 1. Cross 6 under 1 (6 is now 1 and 1 is now 6).

Place 6 over 4.

Place 2 over 6.

Place 1 over 3.

Place 5 over 1.

Repeat steps 2 through 5.

Continue sequence until all strands have been braided.

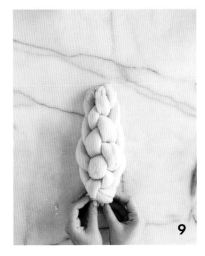

Tuck the ends together to finish the braid.

HONEY BUTTER ROLLS

These rolls are fluffy with just a slight touch of floral sweetness from the honey. The secret to their soft texture is letting them proof until they fill an 8-inch (20-cm) square baking tray and have a texture similar to marshmallows.

MAKES 9 ROLLS

DOUGH

240 g (2 cups) all-purpose flour

120 g (1 cup) bread flour

113 g (½ cup) whole milk, warm

75 g (⅓ cup) water

56 g (3 tbsp) honey

150 g (⅔ cup) active sourdough starter (see page 15)

7 g (1 tsp) salt

57 g (4 tbsp) unsalted butter, cut into 1-inch (2.5-cm) pieces, softened

TOPPING

18 g (1 tbsp) honey

28 g (2 tbsp) unsalted butter

DAY 1

To make the dough, in a large mixing bowl, combine the all-purpose flour, bread flour, milk, water, honey, active starter and salt. Mix until all the flour has been hydrated and the dough is well-combined. Add the butter into the dough 14 grams (1 tablespoon) at a time and mix until it is fully incorporated. Cover the bowl with plastic wrap and allow it to rest for 1 hour.

The dough should feel less sticky, appear smoother and be much easier to work with. Turn it out onto a lightly floured work surface and knead for 5 minutes. Return it to the bowl and cover the bowl with plastic wrap. Place the bowl in a warm place and allow it to rise for 4 to 5 hours, or until your dough has doubled in volume.

Deflate it by pushing down on it, then round it into a tight ball and place it in an airtight container in the refrigerator for an overnight rest.

DAY 2

Line an 8-inch (20-cm) square baking pan with parchment paper. Turn the dough out onto a lightly floured work surface and divide it into nine equal portions. Shape each piece into a tight ball and evenly space each ball in your baking pan. Cover the pan with plastic wrap and a kitchen towel. Set it aside in a warm place and allow the dough to proof for 2 to 4 hours. You'll know the dough is ready to be baked when the balls have doubled in volume, filled the pan and have a texture similar to marshmallows.

Preheat the oven to 350°F (175°C).

In a small microwave-safe bowl, combine the honey and butter and microwave the mixture for 30 seconds to melt the butter. Mix again, then brush the tops of the rolls with the honey butter. Bake for 20 to 25 minutes, or until the rolls are evenly browned. Brush with any leftover honey butter.

These rolls are best served warm. Store any leftovers in an airtight container at room temperature for up to 1 week.

OAT PORRIDGE BROWN BREAD ROLLS

You'll love these rolls on their own or slathered with butter. The oats do double duty, giving these rolls an unbelievably soft texture and a crumb that stays soft and moist for days—plus a crunchy topping.

MAKES 6 ROLLS

OAT PORRIDGE

60 g (½ cup) old-fashioned rolled oats

339 g (1½ cups) whole milk

DOUGH

180 g (1½ cups) whole wheat flour

240 g (2 cups) bread flour

282 g (1¼ cups) warm water

85 g (⅓ cup) active sourdough starter (see page 15)

10 g (1 tbsp) Dutch-process cocoa powder

4 g (2 tsp) instant coffee granules

5 g (¾ tsp) salt

28 g (2 tbsp) unsalted butter

86 g (⅓ cup) honey

30 g (2 tbsp) molasses

30 g (¼ cup) cornmeal

TOPPING

1 egg white, beaten

60 g (½ cup) old-fashioned rolled oats

DAY 1

To make the oat porridge, in a medium saucepan, combine the oats and milk and bring them to a simmer over medium heat. Cook, stirring frequently and adding 14 to 28 grams (1 to 2 tablespoons) of water as needed until the oats are soft and a thick porridge forms, about 3 to 5 minutes. Transfer the porridge to a bowl and set aside to cool completely.

To make the dough, in a large bowl, combine the cooled oat porridge, whole wheat flour, bread flour, water, active starter, cocoa powder, instant coffee, salt, butter, honey and molasses. Stir the ingredients together using a spatula until all the flour has been hydrated and the dough is well-combined. Cover the bowl with plastic wrap and allow the dough to rest for 1 hour.

The dough should feel less sticky, appear smoother and be much easier to work with. Turn it out onto a lightly floured work surface and knead it for 5 minutes. Return it to the bowl, cover with plastic wrap and place in a warm place to rise for 4 to 5 hours, or until your dough has doubled in volume. Deflate the dough by pushing down on it, then round it into a tight ball and place it in an airtight container for an overnight rest in the refrigerator.

DAY 2

Dust a 9 x 13-inch (23 x 33-cm) baking sheet with the cornmeal.

Turn the dough out onto a lightly floured work surface and divide it into six equal portions. Flatten each piece into a 4-inch (10-cm) square. Shape each piece into a mini baguette–style log: fold the top third toward the middle, turn the dough 180 degrees and repeat. Flip the dough seam-side down and drag it toward you to create tension on top. Place the shaped rolls on the baking sheet. Cover the pan with plastic wrap and a kitchen towel and set it aside to proof for 2 to 4 hours, or until the dough has risen and resembles the texture of marshmallows.

Preheat the oven to 350°F (175°C). Brush the tops of the rolls with the egg white and sprinkle the oats evenly on top. Bake for 25 to 30 minutes, or until the interior temperature is 190°F (88°C).

These rolls are best enjoyed warm with a pat of softened butter. Store any leftovers in a ziptop bag at room temperature for up to 1 week.

FLAVORFUL FILLED BREADS AND BUNS

If you're looking to impress your friends and family with your new sourdough baking skills, look no further than these rich, decadent filled breads. Garlic Butter Couronne (page 61), Cherry-Chocolate Babka (page 65) and Sweet Potato–Cardamom Buns (page 62) put a new spin on classic bread recipes. These breads, enriched with eggs and butter and stuffed with rich savory or sweet fillings, are the perfect centerpiece for any dinner party.

GARLIC BUTTER COURONNE

Couronne is French for crown, and both sweet and savory breads are made in this shape, which comes from the Bordeaux region. This couronne is an elegant and delicious alternative to garlic bread. Fragrant garlic and butter fill a highly enriched soft dough, which benefits from extended fermentation.

MAKES 1 LOAF

DOUGH

1 large egg

160 g (¾ cup) whole milk

35 g (2½ tbsp) extra-virgin olive oil

150 g (⅔ cup) active sourdough starter (see page 15)

325 g (2⅔ cups) bread flour

60 g (½ cup) whole wheat flour

28 g (2 tbsp) granulated sugar

7 g (1 tsp) salt

GARLIC BUTTER

6 cloves garlic, crushed

10 g (¾ cup) chopped parsley leaves

57 g (4 tbsp) unsalted butter, softened

15 g (1 tbsp) extra-virgin olive oil

28 g (2 tbsp) unsalted butter, melted

DAY 1

In a large bowl, whisk together the egg, milk, olive oil and active starter until they're fully combined. Stir in the bread flour, whole wheat flour, sugar and salt, and continue mixing until all the flour has been hydrated.

Turn the dough out onto a lightly floured work surface and knead about 10 minutes, until the dough looks smooth. Gather it into a tight ball and place it in a lightly oiled mixing bowl. Cover the bowl with plastic wrap and set it aside at room temperature to rise for 4 to 6 hours, or until the dough has doubled in size.

Deflate it by pushing down on it, then round it into a tight ball and place it in an airtight container in the refrigerator for an overnight rest.

DAY 2

To make the garlic butter, combine the garlic, parsley, softened butter and olive oil in a small bowl and set aside.

Line a 9-inch (23-cm) round cake pan with parchment paper.

On a lightly floured work surface, using a rolling pin, roll the dough out into a 9 x 18-inch (23 x 45-cm) rectangle with the long edge facing you. Spread the garlic butter evenly over the dough. Starting on the long side, roll the dough up tightly, pinching the seam together to seal it. Then cut the rolled dough in half lengthwise, so the filling and layers are exposed. Twist the two pieces of dough around each other and join the ends together to form a circular crown. Pinch the ends to hold them together.

Transfer your couronne to the lined cake pan. Place the pan in a clean plastic bag and leave to proof at room temperature until the dough has doubled, 2 to 4 hours.

Preheat the oven to 350°F (175°C).

Remove the couronne from the plastic bag and brush the top with the melted butter. Bake for 30 to 35 minutes, or until the top is golden brown.

Remove the couronne from your cake pan, peel off the parchment and place the bread on a wire rack to cool for 15 to 20 minutes before serving. This bread is excellent eaten warm. Store any leftovers in a ziptop bag at room temperature for up to 3 days.

SWEET POTATO-CARDAMOM BUNS

My twist on cinnamon buns is enhanced by the richly aromatic flavor of cardamom. Sweet potato imparts a lovely orange hue and locks moisture into the dough, resulting in pillowy soft buns that you won't be able to resist.

MAKES 12 BUNS

DOUGH

360 g (3 cups) all-purpose flour

180 g (1½ cups) bread flour

50 g (¼ cup) granulated sugar

17 g (3 tsp) salt

170 g (¾ cup) active sourdough starter (see page 15)

260 g (1 cup) mashed sweet potatoes, cooled

226 g (1 cup) whole milk

57 g (4 tbsp) unsalted butter, softened

DAY 1

In a large bowl, whisk together the all-purpose flour, bread flour, sugar and salt. In a medium bowl, stir together the active starter, sweet potatoes and milk. Add the sweet potato mixture to the flour mixture and stir all the ingredients together with a spatula or your hands until the dough is fully incorporated.

Knead the dough on a lightly floured work surface for about 5 minutes. Then add the butter 14 grams (1 tablespoon) at a time, kneading each piece into the dough until it's fully incorporated before adding another piece. When all the butter has been added, knead for an additional 10 minutes.

Place the dough in a clean bowl, cover with plastic wrap and allow the dough to rest for 1 hour. Then turn it out onto a lightly floured work surface, knead for 5 minutes and shape it into a tight ball. Place the dough in a lightly oiled bowl, cover with plastic wrap and allow the dough to rise at room temperature until it's almost doubled in volume and appears bubbly, 4 to 6 hours.

Deflate it by pushing down on it, then round it into a tight ball and place it in an airtight container. Refrigerate the dough overnight.

(Continued)

FILLING

215 g (1 cup) brown sugar

40 g (⅓ cup) all-purpose flour

28 g (2 tbsp) unsalted butter, melted

3 g (1 tsp) ground cinnamon

½ tsp ground cardamom

6 g (2 tsp) vanilla extract

CREAM CHEESE GLAZE

84 g (6 tbsp) cream cheese, softened

16 g (2 tbsp) powdered sugar

6 g (½ tbsp) vanilla extract

56 g (¼ cup) whole milk

DAY 2

To make the filling, in a medium bowl, mix the brown sugar, flour, butter, cinnamon, cardamom and vanilla.

Line a 9 x 13–inch (23 x 33–cm) baking pan with parchment paper.

Turn the dough out onto a lightly floured work surface and roll it into an 8 x 24–inch (20 x 60–cm) rectangle, with the longer side facing you. Sprinkle the filling evenly on the dough. Starting with the long side, roll the dough tightly into a log. Using a sharp knife, cut the log into 2-inch (5-cm) segments—you should end up with 12 pieces. Evenly space the buns, cut side up, in the prepared pan, cover with plastic wrap and a kitchen towel and set aside to proof for 2 to 4 hours, or until the dough has doubled in volume and appears puffy, with a marshmallowy texture.

Preheat the oven to 350°F (175°C).

Bake the buns for 20 to 25 minutes, or until they're golden brown. While they bake, mix the glaze. In a small bowl, combine the cream cheese, sugar, vanilla and milk. Remove the buns from the oven and brush with the glaze while they're still hot.

These buns are best served fresh from the oven. Store any leftovers in an airtight container at room temperature for up to 3 days.

CHERRY-CHOCOLATE BABKA

This soft, delicate, cake-like bread is elevated even more by a decadent filling of cherries and chocolate. Creating this bread using a sourdough starter provides much-needed acidity to cut through the rich bitterness of the chocolate filling. Chilling the rolled dough right before cutting makes easy work of shaping.

MAKES 1 LOAF

DOUGH

150 g (⅔ cup) whole milk

300 g (2½ cups) all-purpose flour

6 g (1 tsp) salt

114 g (½ cup) active sourdough starter (see page 15)

1 large egg

FILLING

88 g (⅔ cup) milk chocolate chips

71 g (½ cup) dark chocolate chips

49 g (3½ tbsp) unsalted butter

28 g (2 tbsp) maraschino cherry juice

30 g (¼ cup) powdered sugar

10 maraschino cherries

EGG WASH

1 large egg

14 g (1 tbsp) water

DAY 1

Heat the milk in a small saucepan over low heat, about 2 to 3 minutes. Stir occasionally and be careful not to let the milk boil. Set it aside to cool to room temperature.

In a large mixing bowl, whisk together the flour and salt until they're fully combined and no lumps remain. Add the active starter and egg to the pan with the cooled milk and mix until everything is fully combined. Pour the milk mixture into the flour mixture and stir until all the flour has been fully hydrated. Place the dough in a clean bowl, cover with plastic wrap and set aside to rest for 1 hour.

Turn the dough out onto a lightly floured work surface and knead until it appears smooth, 10 minutes. Gather the dough into a tight ball and transfer it to a lightly oiled bowl. Cover the bowl with plastic wrap and allow the dough to proof until it has doubled, 4 to 6 hours.

Deflate the dough by pushing down on it, then round it into a tight ball and place it in an airtight container. Refrigerate the dough overnight.

DAY 2

Place the milk chocolate and dark chocolate chips and the butter in a microwave-safe bowl and microwave at 50 percent power for 2 minutes, just until the chocolate is melted. Add the maraschino cherry juice and powdered sugar to the chocolate mixture and stir using a spatula until everything is fully combined. Set aside to cool.

(Continued)

Place the dough on a lightly floured work surface and roll it into a 10 x 12–inch (25 x 30.5–cm) rectangle. When the chocolate mixture has cooled, spread it evenly over the dough. Sprinkle the maraschino cherries all over the top. Starting with the short side, roll the dough into a tight log. Pinch the edges to seal the seam. Wrap the cylinder in plastic wrap and refrigerate for about 15 minutes. The dough will be ready to shape when it feels slightly firm to the touch.

Line a 9 x 4½–inch (23 x 11–cm) loaf pan with parchment paper. Unwrap the dough. Using a sharp knife, cut the dough log in half lengthwise. Twist the two pieces together into a 9-inch (23-cm) loaf and place it in the lined loaf pan. Cover the loaf pan with plastic wrap and allow it to rise at room temperature, 2 to 4 hours.

Preheat your oven to 375°F (190°C).

Mix the egg wash by beating the egg and water in a small bowl. Brush the top of the loaf with the egg wash, then bake it for 35 to 40 minutes, or until the loaf is golden brown and the internal temperature is 180°F (82°C).

Remove the loaf from the pan, place on a wire rack and cool for 1 hour before slicing. Store any leftovers in an airtight container at room temperature for up to 3 days.

CHOCOLATE-COCONUT-ALMOND SWIRLS

There's nothing I love more than re-creating my favorite treats with a sourdough twist. This recipe is my take on the iconic candy bar Almond Joy. Adding coconut to the dough gives these soft rolls a delicious and unique texture contrast. You'll bake them in two muffin pans to give the swirls plenty of room to rise and expand.

MAKES 9 BUNS

DOUGH

330 g (2¾ cups) all-purpose flour

60 g (½ cup) bread flour

50 g (½ cup) sweetened coconut flakes

71 g (⅓ cup) granulated sugar

6 g (1 tsp) salt

169 g (¾ cup) active sourdough starter (see page 15)

1 large egg

169 g (¾ cup) coconut milk

57 g (4 tbsp) unsalted butter, softened

ALMOND CREAM

28 g (2 tbsp) unsalted butter, softened

110 g (1 cup) powdered sugar

136 g (1 cup) sliced almonds

1 large egg

7 g (1 tsp) vanilla extract

¼ tsp almond extract

FILLING

100 g (1 cup) sweetened coconut flakes

112 g (⅔ cup) semi-sweet chocolate chips

EGG WASH

1 egg white

14 g (1 tbsp) whole milk

68 g (½ cup) sliced almonds

DAY 1

To make the dough, in a large bowl, combine the all-purpose flour, bread flour, coconut flakes, sugar and salt. Make a well in the center of the mixture and add the active starter, egg and coconut milk. Stir all the ingredients together with a spatula or your hands until the dough is fully incorporated.

Knead the dough on a lightly floured surface for about 5 minutes to develop strength and structure. Then add the butter 14 grams (1 tablespoon) at a time, kneading each piece into the dough until it's fully incorporated before adding another piece. Knead for an additional 10 minutes after all the butter has been added.

Put the dough in a large bowl, cover with plastic wrap and leave it to rest for 1 hour. Turn the dough out onto a lightly floured work surface, knead for 5 minutes and shape it into a tight ball. Place it into a lightly oiled bowl, cover and allow the dough to rise at room temperature until it's almost doubled in volume, 4 to 6 hours.

Deflate the dough by pushing down on it, then round it into a tight ball and place it in an airtight container. Refrigerate the dough overnight.

DAY 2

To make the almond cream, in a food processor, combine the butter, sugar, sliced almonds, egg, vanilla and almond extract, and process until smooth. Set aside.

To make the filling, in a medium bowl, toss together the coconut flakes and chocolate chips. Set aside.

(Continued)

Prepare two 12-cup muffin pans by generously spraying the inside of every other cup with nonstick cooking spray. (You'll spray four cups in one pan and five in the other.)

On a lightly floured work surface, roll the dough out into a 20 x 12-inch (50 x 30-cm) rectangle with the longer side facing you. Spread the almond cream evenly over the dough, then sprinkle the coconut flakes and chocolate chips evenly over the almond cream. Still with the long side facing you, fold the left and right sides of the dough toward the middle, as if you were folding a letter. Using your rolling pin, gently roll the dough out into an 18 x 8-inch (38 x 20-cm) rectangle. With a sharp knife, cut the dough into nine 1 x 8-inch (2.5 x 20-cm) strips. Pick up one strip and hold one end in each hand. Twist the ends in opposite directions, then wrap the twist around three of your fingers and tuck the free end through the hole in the middle, to tie a knot. Place each shaped bun into a prepared cup of the muffin pan. Wrap the muffin pan with plastic wrap and allow the dough to rise for 2 to 4 hours, or until it's doubled in volume.

Preheat your oven to 350°F (175°C).

To make the egg wash, in a small bowl, whisk together the egg white and milk. Brush the egg wash over each of the buns, then sprinkle on the sliced almonds. Bake for 20 to 25 minutes, or until the buns are golden brown.

Cool the buns in the pan for 10 minutes, then remove them to the wire rack to cool completely. Store in a ziptop bag at room temperature for up to 5 days.

BRIOCHE LEMON CUSTARD TART WITH WINE-POACHED PLUMS

There are a lot of moving parts involved in constructing this recipe, but the steps are simpler than they seem and all come together in a dessert that is even greater than the sum of its parts. The custard is simple to make and the soft, buttery, naturally-leavened brioche is a luxurious alternative to regular pie crust.

MAKES 1 LOAF

STIFF ACTIVE SOURDOUGH STARTER

14 g (1 tbsp) sourdough starter

14 g (1 tbsp) warm water

40 g (⅓ cup) all-purpose flour

DOUGH

180 g (1½ cups) all-purpose flour

36 g (2½ tbsp) granulated sugar

4 g (½ tsp) kosher salt

28 g (2 tbsp) whole milk

2 large eggs

84 g (6 tbsp) unsalted butter, room temperature

DAY 1

To make the stiff active sourdough starter, in a large container with an airtight lid, combine the sourdough starter, water and flour. Mix thoroughly. Set aside and allow your starter to activate for about 4 to 6 hours.

To make the dough, in the bowl of a stand mixer fitted with a dough hook, combine the flour, sugar, salt, active starter, milk and eggs, and mix and knead the ingredients together for 10 minutes. (If you don't have a stand mixer, please see my instructions on page 50 for how to knead brioche dough by hand.)

Place the butter between two large pieces of parchment paper and use a rolling pin to flatten and soften it. With the mixer running, add the butter to the dough a little bit at a time. When the butter is fully incorporated, continue mixing the dough until it sticks to the hook and makes a slapping noise against the sides of the bowl, about 5 to 10 minutes.

Gather the dough into a tight ball and place it in a clean bowl. Cover the bowl with plastic wrap and allow it to rise untouched in a warm spot for 4 to 6 hours, or until it has doubled in volume. Deflate it by pushing down on it, then shape it into a tight ball, place it in an airtight container and refrigerate overnight.

(Continued)

CUSTARD

226 g (1 cup) crème fraiche

Zest of 1 lemon

1 large egg

75 g (⅓ cup) granulated sugar

1 egg white, whisked

WINE-POACHED PLUMS

28 g (2 tbsp) water

300 g (1½ cups) granulated sugar

226 g (1 cup) white wine

14 g (1 tbsp) vanilla extract

4 plums, sliced

DAY 2

Line a 10-inch (25-cm) springform cake pan with parchment paper.

Turn the dough out onto a lightly floured work surface and use your hands to flatten it into a 12-inch (30-cm) disk. Carefully transfer the disk to the lined springform pan. Fold and crimp the edges so that there's a ¼-inch (6-mm) gap between the edge of the dough and the springform pan. Wrap the pan in a plastic bag or cover it with plastic wrap and leave it to proof until the dough has doubled in volume and resembles the texture of marshmallows, 2 to 4 hours.

Set a rack in the middle of your oven and preheat it to 275°F (135°C).

To make the custard, in a medium bowl, whisk the crème fraiche, lemon zest and egg together until no streaks remain. Press your fingertips into the brioche dough to flatten the bottom of the tart (not the crimped edges). Pour the custard into the center of the tart, then sprinkle the sugar evenly on top. Brush the egg white on the crimped edges of the crust. Bake for 40 minutes, or until the crust is brown and the custard has set.

While the tart bakes, make the wine sauce. In a small saucepan, combine the water and sugar over medium heat, then bring to a boil; do not stir. As soon as the sugar begins to turn golden in color (about 3 minutes), remove the pan from the heat and add the wine and vanilla. It will sizzle and clump up—don't worry. Return the pan to medium heat, bring the syrup to a boil and continue cooking until the clumps have dissolved, about 5 minutes.

When you're ready to serve, heat the wine sauce in a skillet over medium heat. Add the sliced plums and poach until they're softened, about 2 to 3 minutes. Cut the tart into wedges and top with the warm wine-poached plums and some wine sauce.

The tart should be eaten right away once the poached plums are added. You can store it without the plums in an airtight container in the refrigerator for up to 3 days. Store the wine sauce in a separate container.

FLATBREADS FROM AROUND THE WORLD

Flatbreads have played an important role in the diets and dining tables of people all over the world, long before the discovery of sourdough and the magic of leavening. In this chapter, I'm putting a sourdough twist on some of my favorite flatbread recipes.

Here I've included recipes that use sourdough for its leavening abilities and others that benefit from the complexity of flavor that you simply cannot get using only flour, water and salt. Since each starter comes with its own flavor profile due to the distinctive colony of bacteria and yeast that you've nurtured, the resulting flavors of your flatbreads will be distinct to you. From simple and healthy Whole Wheat Roti (page 82) to hearty Rosemary and Olive Oil Fougasse (page 78) and delicate Scallion Pancakes (page 86), these flatbreads are as unique as the cultures they come from.

RED ONION AND GREEN OLIVE FOCACCIA

With no complicated shaping required, focaccia is one of the easiest breads to master. The key is letting the dough proof properly; otherwise, it will end up flat and dense. Let it bulk until the dough has noticeably increased in volume and is very bubbly. Be creative with toppings—use ingredients from your garden or even some shredded cheese for a pizza-like focaccia.

MAKES 1 FOCACCIA

DOUGH

240 g (2 cups) all-purpose flour

240 g (2 cups) bread flour

376 g (1⅔ cups) warm water

113 g (½ cup) active sourdough starter (see page 15)

15 g (2½ tsp) sea salt

15 g (1 tbsp) extra-virgin olive oil, plus more for rubbing the dough

TOPPING

Extra-virgin olive oil

½ red onion, julienned

10 to 15 green olives, pitted

Coarse sea salt

DAY 1

In a large mixing bowl, combine the all-purpose flour, bread flour, water, active starter and salt. Mix the ingredients together using your hands or a wooden spoon until all the flour is hydrated and well combined. Stretch and fold the dough until it appears smooth. When it feels smooth, stretchy and strong, add the olive oil and fold until it's fully incorporated. Cover the bowl with plastic wrap and allow the dough to rest for 1 hour.

During bulk fermentation, complete three or four stretch and folds at 30-minute intervals, depending on how the dough feels. When you're done, your dough should look very smooth, feel only slightly tacky and pass the windowpane test (page 23). Cover the bowl with plastic wrap and allow the dough to bulk ferment for 2 to 4½ hours, or until it appears bubbly and has doubled in volume.

Line a 9 x 13-inch (23 x 33-cm) baking sheet with parchment paper. Shape your dough into a batard (page 25), rub the dough with olive oil, cover the pan with plastic wrap and refrigerate overnight.

DAY 2

Preheat your oven to 500°F (260°C).

Take the baking sheet with the dough out of the refrigerator. Rub more olive oil on the surface of the dough and use the tips of your fingers to dimple the dough all over, being careful not to poke holes in it. Top the dough with the onion and olives, and finish with a sprinkling of sea salt.

Bake for 20 to 25 minutes, or until the focaccia is golden brown throughout with only a few dark spots. Take it out of the oven and let it cool for 15 minutes before cutting. Focaccia is best enjoyed warm.

Wrap any leftover bread in foil and store at room temperature for up to 5 days. Reheat wrapped in foil at 350°F (175°C) for 10 minutes.

ROSEMARY AND OLIVE OIL FOUGASSE

Never to be upstaged, the French version of flatbread is beautifully shaped like an ear of wheat, with a large proportion of hearty crust. Traditionally flavored with fresh herbs, this bread is best dipped in olive oil and balsamic vinegar and served alongside lovely soft cheeses.

MAKES 2 FOUGASSE

120 g (1 cup) whole wheat flour

360 g (3 cups) bread flour

376 g (1⅔ cups) warm water

113 g (½ cup) active sourdough starter (see page 15)

4 g (2 tbsp) chopped fresh rosemary

12 g (2 tsp) sea salt

15 g (1 tbsp) extra-virgin olive oil

DAY 1

In a large mixing bowl, combine the whole wheat flour, bread flour, water, active starter, rosemary and salt. Mix the ingredients together until all the flour is hydrated. Fold the dough until it appears smooth and has built some strength. Add the oil and continue folding until it's fully incorporated. Cover the bowl with plastic wrap and allow the dough to rest for 1 hour.

During bulk fermentation, complete three or four stretch and folds at 30-minute intervals, until your dough passes the windowpane test (page 23). Cover the bowl with plastic wrap and allow the dough to ferment for 2 to 3 hours, or until it has increased in volume 30 to 50 percent.

Cut two large pieces of parchment paper and place them side by side on an 18 x 13-inch (46 x 33-cm) baking sheet. Divide the dough in half, shape each piece into a tight ball and place each ball on a piece of parchment paper. Cover the baking sheet with plastic wrap and place it in the refrigerator overnight.

DAY 2

Put a pizza stone or an 18 x 13-inch (45 x 33-cm) baking sheet on the middle rack of the oven and a deep baking pan on the bottom rack. Preheat the oven to 500°F (260°C). Bring 1 cup (240 ml) of water to a boil.

Working with one ball of dough at a time, lift the dough on the parchment paper and place it on your work surface. Flatten the dough out into an oval using a rolling pin. Using a pizza cutter or a bench scraper, make two vertical cuts (each about 3 to 4 inches [7 to 10 cm] long) all the way through the middle of the dough and four horizontal cuts (each about 2 to 3 inches [5 to 7 cm] long) on each side of the dough. Open the cuts up using your fingers so that the holes do not close.

Transfer the dough on the parchment paper onto the hot pizza stone or baking sheet. Pour the hot water into the baking pan inside the oven. Bake for 20 minutes with steam, then remove the baking pan and continue baking for another 10 minutes until the bread is browned.

Move the bread to a wire rack and allow it to cool about 20 minutes before serving. Bake the first fougasse all the way through, then bake the second one.

These are best enjoyed freshly baked. Wrap any leftover bread in foil and store at room temperature for up to 1 week. Reheat at 350°F (175°C) wrapped in foil for 15 minutes.

SESAME-POPPY SEED BARBARI BREAD

Originally from Iran, this flatbread encrusted with seeds is crispy on the outside with a thick, fluffy crumb—perfect for dipping in olive oil. The key to achieving the beautifully crusty exterior is the roomal glaze. This bread is delicious served warm with olives, olive oil and feta cheese.

MAKES 2 FLATBREADS

DOUGH

480 g (4 cups) bread flour

380 g (1½ cups) warm water

150 g (⅔ cup) active sourdough starter (see page 15)

9 g (1½ tsp) sea salt

ROOMAL GLAZE

7 g (2 tsp) all-purpose flour

3 g (½ tsp) sugar

2 g (½ tsp) vegetable oil

70 g (⅓ cup) water

TOPPING

3 g (1 tsp) poppy seeds

3 g (1 tsp) white sesame seeds

4 g (½ tsp) coarse sea salt

DAY 1

In a large bowl, combine the flour, water, active starter and salt, and mix until all the flour is thoroughly hydrated and well combined. Fold the dough until it appears smooth. Cover the bowl with plastic wrap and allow the dough to rest for 1 hour.

During bulk fermentation, complete three or four stretch and folds at 30-minute intervals, until your dough passes the windowpane test (page 23). Cover the bowl with plastic wrap and allow the dough to ferment for 2 to 2½ hours, until it has increased in volume 30 to 50 percent.

Cut two large pieces of parchment paper and place them side by side on an 18 x 13–inch (46 x 33–cm) baking sheet. Divide the dough in half, shape each piece into a tight ball and place each ball on a piece of parchment paper. Cover the baking sheet with plastic wrap and place it in the refrigerator overnight.

DAY 2

Put a pizza stone or an 18 x 13–inch (45 x 33–cm) baking sheet in the middle rack of the oven and preheat the oven to 500°F (260°C).

To make the glaze, in a small saucepan combine the flour, sugar, oil and water. Bring the mixture to a boil, then cook over medium heat, stirring constantly, until it is thick enough to coat a spoon, about 1 minute. Remove the pan from the heat and set aside.

Working with one piece of dough at a time, slide a piece of dough, still on the parchment paper, onto your work surface. Gently deflate the dough and flatten it into a 12 x 6–inch (30 x 15–cm) rectangle. Using your fingers, press five ridges along the surface of the dough lengthwise, making sure you press firmly but do not puncture the dough. Brush half the glaze evenly over the surface of the dough, then sprinkle half the poppy seeds, sesame seeds and coarse salt on top.

Carefully slide the dough, still on the paper, onto the hot stone and bake it for 15 to 20 minutes, or until it's golden brown. Remove the bread from the oven and transfer to a wire rack to cool. Repeat the process with the second piece of dough.

Serve warm. Store any leftovers wrapped in foil for up to 1 week at room temperature.

WHOLE WHEAT ROTI

Made with whole wheat, without fat or leaveners, roti are healthy, delicious and easy to prepare. A flat-bottomed pan or skillet works perfectly to cook them on the stovetop. Finish these directly over an open flame to give them a fabulous charred flavor. Enjoy with a delicious Indian curry dish, chutney or even as a sandwich wrap.

MAKES 10 ROTI

180 g (1½ cups) whole wheat flour, divided

6 g (1 tsp) coarse sea salt or kosher salt

113 g (½ cup) hot water

56 g (¼ cup) sourdough discard

DAY 1

In a large bowl, whisk together 145 grams (1¼ cups) of flour and the salt until no lumps remain. Create a well in the center of the flour and add the hot water. Stir with a wooden spoon until the mixture forms a shaggy dough. Be careful—the mixture may be extremely hot! Set the dough aside and allow it to cool to room temperature.

Add the sourdough discard and mix it in with a wooden spoon. If the mixture feels too wet, add an extra 25 grams (¼ cup) of flour. Turn the dough out onto a lightly floured work surface and knead it until it's smooth, about 5 to 10 minutes.

Sprinkle a little of the leftover flour on a large plate. Divide the dough into ten equal pieces and roll each piece into a ball. Roll each ball in the flour on the plate to coat and flatten it slightly. Place all the dough pieces on the floured plate and cover with a damp kitchen towel. Set aside for at least 1 hour so the gluten can relax.

On a lightly floured work surface, use a rolling pin to flatten each piece of dough into a 6-inch (15-cm) disk. The dough should be easier to roll out at this point, but if it snaps back, allow it to rest for another 15 minutes. The disks you roll out should be almost paper thin. Dust each disk liberally with flour; you should be able to stack the dough disks without them sticking to one another.

Heat a medium nonstick skillet over medium-high heat. Cook each roti for 30 seconds on each side, flipping when you begin to see small dark spots on the surface of the dough.

Remove the roti from the skillet and, using a long pair of tongs, place it directly over the gas flame, cooking until it puffs up like a balloon. Flip it back and forth until you see charred spots all over. If you don't have a gas stove, a wire rack positioned on top of your electric burner or your outdoor barbecue grill works just as well.

Transfer the roti to a serving dish and cover it with a kitchen towel to keep it warm while you cook the rest. Serve immediately.

Store any leftovers in an airtight container in the refrigerator for 3 days or in the freezer for up to a month. Reheat the roti by grilling them for a few seconds.

FLOUR TORTILLAS

Fresh flour tortillas are far superior to anything you can buy at the store. Plus, making them takes just about as long as a trip to the grocery store. A cast-iron skillet works well for these tortillas, if you have one. Sourdough discard gives these tortillas a hearty tang that makes them taste as if they went through a lengthy fermentation.

MAKES 8 TORTILLAS

180 g (1½ cups) all-purpose flour

3 g (½ tsp) salt

7 g (1 tsp) baking powder

20 g (1 tbsp) lard or vegetable oil

113 g (½ cup) sourdough discard

56 g (¼ cup) hot water

DAY 1

In a medium bowl, combine the flour, salt and baking powder. Using your fingers, rub the lard into the dry ingredients until the mixture resembles pea-sized crumbs. Add the sourdough discard and water, working the liquid into the flour using a wooden spoon until the mixture comes together into a ball of dough.

Allow the dough to cool slightly, then knead for 5 to 10 minutes until it becomes smooth and pliable. (The dough should not be sticky at this point, so you shouldn't need to dust your work surface with flour.) Wrap the dough in plastic wrap and let it rest for at least 30 minutes or in the refrigerator overnight.

Divide the dough into eight equal portions, roll each into a tight ball and cover the pieces of dough with a damp kitchen towel. Allow the dough to rest for 15 to 30 minutes.

Using a rolling pin, roll each piece of dough into an 8-inch (20-cm) disk. At this point, you can start cooking the tortillas or stack them with a piece of parchment paper between each one to cook later.

Heat a heavy-bottomed skillet over high heat and cook the tortillas one at a time for 30 seconds on each side, or until the dough looks dry and a few brown spots form on the surface. Do not overcook or they will be hard and crispy instead of soft and pliable.

Transfer the tortilla to a serving dish and cover with a kitchen towel to keep it warm while you cook the rest. Serve immediately.

Store leftover tortillas in an airtight container in the refrigerator for a week or in the freezer for up to a month. Reheat directly over an open flame or on a hot skillet for 1 minute.

SCALLION PANCAKES

These scallion pancakes are flaky and crispy on the outside, with a chewy interior. Unlike conventional pancakes, which are made with batter, these are made with dough. Their flakiness comes from rolling the dough into a membrane-like sheet and then rolling it into itself to create beautiful, thin layers.

MAKES 6 PANCAKES

PANCAKE DOUGH

240 g (2 cups) all-purpose flour

60 g (½ cup) cornstarch

3 g (½ tsp) Chinese five-spice powder

3 g (½ tsp) salt

56 g (¼ cup) sourdough discard

113 g (½ cup) boiling water

14 g (1 tbsp) toasted sesame oil

56 g (¼ cup) melted lard or vegetable oil

3 scallions, thinly sliced

56 to 84 g (4 to 6 tbsp) vegetable oil

DIPPING SAUCE

28 g (2 tbsp) soy sauce

1 scallion, thinly sliced

8 g (2 tsp) rice vinegar

4 g (1 tsp) honey

4 g (1 tsp) toasted sesame oil

Pinch of red pepper flakes

DAY 1

Whisk together the flour, cornstarch, five-spice powder and salt in a large mixing bowl until no lumps remain. Make a well in the center and add the sourdough discard, water and sesame oil. Work the wet ingredients into the flour mixture until everything is fully combined and forms a dough. Cover the bowl with a damp kitchen towel and allow the dough to rest for 15 minutes.

Knead the dough for 5 to 10 minutes until it's extremely smooth and pliable. (The dough should not be sticky at this point and you should not need to dust your work surface with flour.) Return the dough to the bowl and cover with the kitchen towel. Allow the dough to rest for another 30 minutes. This rest period will let the gluten relax and will make it easier to roll out the dough.

While you're waiting, make the dipping sauce. In a small serving bowl, combine the soy sauce, scallion, vinegar, honey, sesame oil and red pepper flakes.

Divide the dough into six equal portions. Flatten each piece of dough and then roll it into a large round circle; rolling the dough as thin as possible will result in flakier pancakes. Brush each piece with melted lard and sprinkle some scallions evenly on top. Roll up the circle into a long rope, then twist it into a spiral. Repeat until you've prepared all the dough portions. Use your hands to flatten each piece into a 6-inch (15-cm) disk about ⅛ inch (3 mm) thick.

Heat 1 tablespoon (15 ml) of vegetable oil in a small skillet over medium-high heat. Cook one pancake at a time until it's golden brown, about 2 to 3 minutes on each side. Set the pancake on a serving plate and cover it with a kitchen towel to keep warm while you are cooking the rest.

These pancakes are best eaten immediately after cooking. Enjoy them warm with dipping sauce.

For long-term storage, place pieces of parchment paper between flattened uncooked pancakes. Store them in an airtight container in the freezer for up to 1 month. Cook the frozen pancakes the same way you would fresh ones, although the cooking time may be slightly longer.

FOCACCIA DI RECCO

This cheese-stuffed flatbread is less well known than other famous Italian breads, but it's every bit as delicious. Traditional Focaccia di Recco is made with a soft cheese called *crescenza*, which can be a bit hard to find in American grocery stores. A melty cheese such as brie is more widely available and is a great alternative.

MAKES 1 FOCACCIA

DOUGH

77 g (⅓ cup) water

28 g (2 tbsp) extra-virgin olive oil

113 g (½ cup) sourdough discard

210 g (1¾ cups) bread flour

6 g (1 tsp) kosher salt

FILLING AND TOPPING

250 g (1 cup) sliced brie cheese

Extra-virgin olive oil

Coarse sea salt

20 g (1 cup) arugula

Parmesan cheese (optional)

DAY 1

In a small bowl, combine the water, olive oil and sourdough discard and stir to dissolve. Put the flour and salt in a large bowl, make a well in the middle of the flour and pour the dissolved starter into the well. Using a fork, incorporate the flour, little by little, until all the flour has become hydrated and the mixture begins coming together into a shaggy dough.

Knead the dough for 5 to 10 minutes until it appears smooth. (The dough should not be sticky at this point and you should not need to dust your work surface with flour.) Wrap the dough in plastic wrap and allow it to rest at room temperature for 1 hour or in the refrigerator overnight.

When you're ready to bake, preheat the oven to 400°F (200°C). Grease a 9 x 13–inch (23 x 33–cm) baking sheet with olive oil.

Divide the dough in half. Working with one portion at a time, roll the dough out into a 10-inch (25-cm) square. Place the square on your greased baking sheet and carefully stretch one edge of the dough over the edge of the baking sheet; the dough should hang off and cling to the top edge of the baking sheet. Continue stretching until your dough covers the entire baking sheet and hangs over the sides. Be careful not to tear it. Place the brie slices evenly on top of the stretched dough.

Roll out the other piece of dough into a square. Place it on top of the cheese layer and stretch until it covers the whole pan. Roll your rolling pin around the edges of the baking sheet to stick together the two layers of dough and to remove any excess overhanging dough. Seal the focaccia completely by pinching and rolling the edges of the dough. Pinch a few holes into the top layer of dough above the cheese to release steam during baking. Brush the top of the focaccia with olive oil and finish with a sprinkling of sea salt.

Bake the focaccia for 7 to 10 minutes, or until the cheese is bubbly and the flatbread appears evenly browned. When the focaccia is done, remove it from the oven and let it cool slightly before cutting it into pieces. Enjoy it warm, topped with fresh arugula and a drizzle of olive oil and Parmesan cheese, if desired.

Wrap any leftovers in aluminum foil and store in the refrigerator for up to 2 days. Reheat in a hot oven for 3 to 5 minutes.

FERMENTED PASTA, NOODLES AND DUMPLINGS

The recipes in this chapter are among the ones I'm most proud of creating, because they are probably the most unexpected. I love finding inventive ways to incorporate sourdough discard into my cooking, and I always shock people when I tell them that the Semolina Egg Pasta (page 93) or the Pork-Ginger Gyoza (page 97) they are enjoying has sourdough in it. You can prepare the dough and serve these dishes in under 2 hours. Alternatively, giving the dough an overnight rest in the refrigerator allows you to take advantage of the benefits of a long fermentation, making the pasta easier to digest, especially for those with gluten sensitivities.

SEMOLINA EGG PASTA

Equal proportions of semolina flour and all-purpose flour result in a tender pasta with a tasty little tang that's easier to digest than other fresh pastas because of the sourdough discard. To take full advantage of its benefits, let your pasta dough ferment for a full 24 hours instead of just 2. Fermented or not, though, the sourdough adds a complexity of flavor that is delicious with any pasta sauce. I roll out and cut this pasta using a pasta machine, but you can do it by hand using a rolling pin.

SERVES 4

120 g (1 cup) all-purpose flour

120 g (1 cup) fine semolina flour

6 g (1 tsp) kosher salt

113 g (½ cup) sourdough discard

2 large eggs

DAY 1

In a large bowl, combine the all-purpose flour, semolina flour and salt. Make a well in the center and add the sourdough discard and eggs. Using a fork, break up the egg yolks and incorporate the flour, little by little, until a paste forms.

Turn the dough out onto a work surface and continue adding any unincorporated flour until your mixture forms a ball of dough. It may take a few minutes until all the flour is hydrated and you have a cohesive dough.

Once your dough forms, knead it for about 10 to 15 minutes, until it appears smooth and elastic with only a few cracks. Kneading your dough will impart structure to your pasta and ensure your noodles will not break apart when cooked. Cover the dough with plastic wrap and allow it to rest at room temperature for at least 2 hours. After this initial rest period, you can take advantage of the fermentation benefits of sourdough by placing your wrapped pasta dough in the refrigerator and allowing it to ferment for up to 2 days. Or you can cut the dough right after its 2-hour rest.

When you're ready to cut your pasta, sprinkle a generous amount of flour on a large baking sheet and set it aside.

Use a sharp knife to cut your dough into four equal portions. Place one wedge on a floured work surface and immediately wrap the remaining three in plastic wrap to prevent them from drying out. Using a rolling pin, roll the dough wedge into a rectangle that is thin enough to go through the widest setting on your pasta machine.

Liberally flour the dough and feed it through your pasta machine on its widest setting. When the sheet comes out, fold it into thirds. Repeat once or twice more. Then continue to feed the dough through the machine as you gradually reduce the settings, one pass at a time, until you get to the third thinnest setting. Dust the dough with more flour if it feels sticky as you go, and if your dough gets too long to handle, simply use a knife to cut it in half. Set the sheet of rolled-out pasta dough on the prepared baking sheet and cover it with plastic wrap to prevent it from drying out. Repeat this process with the rest of the dough portions.

Attach the cutter attachment to your pasta machine (choose any size noodles you like). Liberally flour one sheet of pasta and carefully feed it through the cutter attachment. Once cut, dust the noodles with flour to prevent them from sticking together. Swirl the noodles into a nest and return them to the floured baking sheet. Repeat until all the pasta sheets have been cut.

Cook the pasta in a pot of well-salted boiling water for 90 seconds. You can also freeze the uncooked pasta nests uncovered for 30 minutes and then transfer them to a ziptop bag. They will keep for up to 1 month. You don't need to adjust the cooking time when preparing frozen pasta.

RAMEN NOODLES

Once you have eaten homemade ramen noodles, you'll be utterly spoiled. And because they are so easy to make, you may never buy ramen again. These ramen noodles get their chew from bread flour and the addition of baked baking soda to the dough. You can bake a large batch of baking soda in advance and use it whenever you want fresh ramen.

SERVES 2 TO 4

BAKED BAKING SODA

60 g (½ cup) baking soda

DOUGH

7 g (2 tsp) baked baking soda

4 g (½ tsp) salt

56 g (¼ cup) hot water

180 g (1½ cups) bread flour

113 g (½ cup) sourdough discard

Cornstarch

DAY 1

To bake the baking soda, preheat your oven to 250°F (120°C). Spread the baking soda on a baking sheet and bake for 1 hour. Allow the baking soda to cool completely and store it in an airtight container until you're ready to use it.

To make the dough, in a small bowl, dissolve the baked baking soda and salt in the hot water.

In a large bowl, combine the flour and sourdough discard, and stir to incorporate. Add the baking soda and water mixture and knead the dough in the bowl until everything is fully combined, about 5 minutes. Wrap the dough in plastic wrap and allow it to rest for 30 minutes.

Knead the dough for another 10 minutes. Divide it in half, shape each piece into a log and wrap both in plastic wrap. Allow the dough to rest for 1 hour; this will let the gluten relax and make it easier to handle. You can refrigerate the uncut dough for up to 24 hours, although it may turn a little gray.

When you're ready to cut your noodles, sprinkle a generous amount of cornstarch on a baking sheet and set it aside. Working with one portion at a time, flatten the log using a rolling pin until the dough will fit into your pasta machine. The dough may break apart the first time you run it through your pasta machine; that's okay. Just fold it into thirds and continue rolling it on the widest setting until you end up with a smooth pasta dough.

Then continue to feed the dough through the machine as you gradually reduce the settings, one pass at a time, until you get to the third thinnest setting. If your dough gets too long to handle, simply use a knife to cut it in half. Set the sheet of rolled-out pasta dough on the prepared baking sheet and cover it with plastic wrap to prevent it from drying out. Repeat this process with the other dough portion.

Attach the cutter attachment to your machine, dust each sheet with cornstarch and carefully feed it through the cutter on the angel hair setting. Once cut, dust the noodles with cornstarch to prevent them from sticking together. Swirl them into a nest and return them to the baking sheet.

Cook the noodles in a pot of well-salted boiling water for 90 seconds.

You can also freeze the uncooked pasta nests uncovered for 30 minutes and then transfer them to a ziptop bag. They will keep for up to 1 month. You don't need to adjust the cooking time when preparing frozen pasta.

PORK-GINGER GYOZA

Making dumpling wrappers from scratch is easier than you think! Using a pasta machine makes quick work of rolling the thin sheets of dough if you want gyoza with a more delicate wrapper, or opt for a thicker wrapper if you want something a bit more substantial. Make sure you knead this dough thoroughly to build strength and structure, or the wrappers will be too soft and difficult to shape.

MAKES 38 GYOZA

DUMPLING WRAPPERS

113 g (½ cup) sourdough discard

240 g (2 cups) all-purpose flour

113 g (½ cup) hot water

5 g (⅔ tsp) kosher salt

Cornstarch

FILLING

453 g (1 lb) napa cabbage, finely diced

14 g (1 tbsp + ½ tsp) kosher salt, divided

453 g (1 lb) ground pork

75 g (½ cup) finely diced carrots

10 g (1 tbsp) minced garlic

2 g (1 tsp) grated fresh ginger

100 g (⅔ cup) finely diced onions

50 g (1 cup) finely diced shiitake mushrooms

5 g (1 tsp) toasted sesame oil

5 g (1 tsp) ground white pepper

9 g (2 tsp) granulated sugar

28 g (2 tbsp) grapeseed or vegetable oil

OPTIONAL TOPPINGS

Soy sauce

Chili oil

DAY 1

To make the dumpling wrappers, in a medium bowl, combine the sourdough discard, flour, water and salt. Use your hands to mix the ingredients until they form a shaggy dough. Knead the dough on a lightly floured surface until it forms a homogenous mass and appears smooth, around 10 minutes. Place the dough in an airtight container and allow it to rest for at least 1 hour at room temperature or up to 48 hours in the refrigerator. The longer you allow your dough to rest, the easier it will be to roll out.

The easiest way to roll out these dumpling wrappers is to use a pasta machine. Lightly flour your work surface and divide the dough into three portions. Flatten each piece of dough into a 4-inch (10-cm) square (measurements do not have to be exact). Roll the dough through your machine until you reach the second thinnest setting. Cut the dough using a 4-inch (10-cm) round cookie cutter. Reroll any remaining scraps of dough. Dust the wrappers with cornstarch, stack and cover with plastic wrap until you're ready to assemble your gyoza.

To make the filling, put the cabbage in a large mixing bowl, toss with 4 grams (½ teaspoon) of salt and set aside for 15 minutes. Drain the cabbage, squeezing out as much water as possible.

In a large bowl, combine the drained cabbage, remaining 10 grams (1 tablespoon) of salt, pork, carrots, garlic, ginger, onions, mushrooms, sesame oil, white pepper and sugar. Stir all the ingredients together until the filling is well combined and feels sticky, about 5 minutes.

(Continued)

Set a small bowl of water next to your work surface and begin making the dumplings. Place a small dab of filling (about a third of the size of the wrapper) into the middle of one wrapper. Dip your finger in the water and lightly wet the edges of the wrapper. Fold the wrapper in half and seal it by pinching the edges together, then bring the two ends together to form a rosebud shape. Repeat until you have used up all your wrappers and filling.

Place the grapeseed oil in a medium frying pan over medium-high heat. Arrange the gyoza flat side down in a single layer in the pan and fry for 2 minutes. Pour about 28 grams (2 tablespoons) of water into the pan and cover. Steam for 5 to 6 minutes, adding a little more water if it evaporates too quickly. Serve the gyoza warm with soy sauce and chili oil.

If you're making the gyoza ahead of time, place each on a parchment paper–lined baking sheet and freeze in a single layer. When they are completely frozen, place the gyoza in a ziptop bag and store them in the freezer for up to 2 months. Cook them frozen as described above, but add 1 to 2 minutes to the cooking time.

POTATO-CHEDDAR-CHIVE PIEROGI

These little dumplings are the perfect recipe for potato lovers. Adding sourdough discard to the dumpling wrapper results in an airier dough, thanks to carbon dioxide from the yeast, which makes for a lighter pierogi. Shaping 30 pierogi may seem like a lot of work, but this dough is so fun to work with that it won't feel tedious at all. Plus, you'll be glad to have plenty of frozen pierogi that can be whipped up as a quick snack.

MAKES 30 PIEROGI

DOUGH

180 g (1½ cups) bread flour

3 g (½ tsp) baking powder

4 g (½ tsp) kosher salt

113 g (½ cup) sourdough discard

56 g (¼ cup) whole milk

1 large egg

FILLING

226 g (½ cup) mashed potatoes, warm

63 g (¼ cup) grated cheddar cheese

28 g (2 tbsp) unsalted butter, room temperature

6 g (2 tbsp) finely chopped chives

5 g (¾ tsp) kosher salt

¼ tsp ground black pepper

TOPPING

28 g (2 tbsp) unsalted butter

½ large onion, sliced

28 g (2 tbsp) crème fraiche or sour cream

Scallions (optional)

DAY 1

To make the dough, in a large bowl, whisk together the flour, baking powder and salt. Add the sourdough discard, milk and egg, and stir the ingredients together until the mixture forms a dough.

Turn the dough out onto a work surface and knead for 10 to 15 minutes, or until it is smooth and elastic. Round the dough into a ball and place it in a clean bowl. Cover with plastic wrap and refrigerate until you are ready to assemble the dumplings. This dough will keep well in the refrigerator for up to 2 days.

To make the filling, in a large bowl, add the mashed potatoes, cheddar cheese, butter, chives, salt and pepper. Mix vigorously. You can do this with an electric handheld mixer, in the bowl of a stand mixer or by hand. Just make sure the cheese and butter are fully melted and incorporated (that's why it's important that your potatoes are warm when you mix your filling). Spread the filling in a shallow dish to fully cool before assembling.

Line a rimmed baking sheet with parchment paper and dust it with flour.

(Continued)

Roll the dough out on a floured work surface until it is about an ⅛ inch (3 mm) thick. Using a 3-inch (7.5-cm) biscuit cutter, cut as many circles as you can from the dough (about 20 to 25). Place about 14 grams (1 tablespoon) of cooled filling in the center of each disk. Fold the dough in half over the filling to create a half-moon shape and pinch the edges firmly to seal. Transfer the pierogi to the prepared sheet. Reroll the dough with any cut scraps until your filling runs out (rerolling this dough will not affect the texture of your pierogi). Cover the pierogi with plastic wrap and refrigerate them until you're ready to cook, up to 3 hours.

Cook your pierogi in well-salted boiling water for 5 minutes. Don't be tempted to pull them out of the water when they start to float; you may end up with uncooked dough if you pull them out of the water before 5 minutes are up. Drain and set aside.

To finish them, melt the butter in a large skillet over medium heat. Sauté the onion in the butter until it begins to brown, about 2 minutes. Add the drained pierogi and cook until they're browned and crisped, about 3 minutes. Serve hot topped with crème fraîche and scallions, if desired.

If you're not cooking them right away, freeze the pierogi flat on the baking sheet, then transfer them to a ziptop bag. Store in the freezer for up to 1 month. Cook them frozen as described above.

BASIL RAVIOLI WITH SUNDRIED TOMATO-RICOTTA FILLING

Basil lends a beautiful green hue and peppery notes to the sourdough in this fermented pasta. These ravioli taste great with tomato sauce or just a little olive oil and Parmesan cheese.

MAKES 20 TO 24 RAVIOLI

DOUGH

7 g (¼ cup) basil leaves

113 g (½ cup) sourdough discard

2 large eggs

240 g (2 cups) all-purpose flour

¼ tsp salt

FILLING

292 g (1½ cups) full-fat ricotta

1 large egg

45 g (½ cup) diced sundried tomatoes

90 g (1 cup) grated Parmesan cheese

5 g (¾ tsp) kosher salt

3 g (½ tsp) ground black pepper

DAY 1

In a blender, mix the basil, sourdough discard and eggs together until the leaves are liquefied. In a large bowl, combine the flour and salt, and add the mixture from the blender. Mix until a dough forms. Turn the dough out onto a work surface and continue adding any unincorporated flour until your mixture forms a ball of dough. Wrap the dough in plastic wrap and allow it to ferment at room temperature for 1 hour or in the refrigerator for up to 48 hours.

While you're waiting, make the filling. In a large bowl, mix the ricotta, egg, sundried tomatoes, Parmesan cheese, salt and pepper until thoroughly combined. Cover and set aside while you roll out the pasta dough.

Dust a baking sheet with flour and set aside. Use a sharp knife to cut your dough into six equal portions. Place one portion on a work surface and immediately wrap the remaining portions in plastic wrap to prevent them from drying out.

Liberally flour the dough and feed it through your pasta machine on its widest setting. When the sheet comes out, fold it in thirds. Repeat once or twice more. Then continue to feed the dough through the machine as you gradually reduce the settings, one pass at a time, until you get to the third thinnest setting. Dust the dough with more flour if it feels sticky as you go, and cut your dough in half if it gets too long to handle. Place the rolled-out dough on the prepared baking sheet and cover it with plastic wrap to keep it from drying out. Repeat this process with the rest of the dough portions.

To assemble your ravioli, place one sheet of pasta on a lightly floured surface with the long side facing you. Mound 7 grams (1 teaspoon) of filling on the dough, leaving a 1-inch (2.5-cm) margin from the edges of the dough. Continue placing spoonfuls of ricotta filling in a row, leaving 2 inches (5 cm) between each one and keeping an even 1 inch (2.5 cm) from the bottom edge. Lightly brush the dough all around the filling with water. Place another sheet of dough on top and gently press it around the filling to seal. Using a ravioli stamp or a sharp knife, cut the filled dough into 2-inch (5-cm) square ravioli. Place the ravioli on the prepared baking sheet and cover with plastic wrap until you're done making them all.

Cook the ravioli in a pot of well-salted boiling water for 90 seconds. If you're not cooking them right away, freeze the ravioli flat on the baking sheet, then transfer them to a ziptop bag. Store in the freezer for up to 1 month. Cook them frozen in well-salted boiling water for 90 seconds to 2 minutes.

CRISPY CRACKERS AND BREADSTICKS

This is where sourdough discard really shines. The perfect solution to an overflowing discard jar, these recipes use a lot of discard, are quick to make and keep for up to a month. These crackers are crispy, with a characteristic tang that you can only achieve with sourdough. Buttery Charcoal Crackers (page 107) and Sage-Onion Grissini (page 112) will elevate any cheese plate, while homemade Spelt and Einkorn Graham Crackers (page 115) make for the perfect sweet snack—or a graham cracker crumb pie crust.

BUTTERY CHARCOAL CRACKERS

Buttery and crispy, these charcoal crackers make for a striking accompaniment to luscious blue cheese. Due to the charcoal powder added to the dough, it can be hard to judge the doneness of these crackers. They should appear bluish gray at the end of the bake; if they turn brown, you've gone too long. Adding more charcoal powder will help you achieve a darker hue but will result in a grittier texture. You can find activated charcoal powder at drug stores, health food stores and online.

MAKES 30 TO 40 CRACKERS

60 g (½ cup) all-purpose flour

4 g (½ tsp) activated charcoal powder

¼ tsp baking powder

7 g (½ tbsp) granulated sugar

¼ tsp coarse sea salt or Himalayan salt

42 g (3 tbsp) unsalted butter, cold, cut into pieces

113 g (½ cup) sourdough discard

12 g (1 tbsp) vegetable oil

DAY 1

In a medium mixing bowl, sift the flour, charcoal powder, baking powder, sugar and salt. Using a pastry cutter or two butter knives, incorporate the chilled butter into the flour until the mixture resembles coarse crumbs. Stir in the sourdough discard and vegetable oil until the mixture is fully incorporated.

Turn the dough out onto a piece of plastic wrap. Using the plastic wrap, bring the dough together and knead gently for a few seconds, or until it forms a cohesive ball. Wrap the dough tightly and place it in the refrigerator to chill for 30 minutes.

Preheat the oven to 400°F (200°C).

Divide the dough in half. Working with one portion at a time, place the dough between two pieces of parchment paper. Use a rolling pin to roll it out until it is ⅛ inch (3 mm) thick. Peel off the top piece of parchment and prick the dough all over with a fork to prevent it from puffing up in the oven. Using a pizza slicer, cut the dough into 2-inch (5-cm) squares, but do not break the squares apart yet. Transfer the dough sheet, still on the parchment paper, to a 9 x 13-inch (23 x 33-cm) baking sheet. Repeat with the second piece of dough on a second baking sheet.

Bake the crackers for 5 to 10 minutes. Watch them closely to ensure they do not burn. With the baking sheets still in the oven, turn the oven off and keep the door slightly ajar to help the crackers air dry and crisp up, about 10 to 15 minutes.

Remove the crackers from the oven and allow them to cool completely. Once cooled, snap the crackers apart along the scored lines. Store the cooled crackers in an airtight container for up to 1 month.

MANCHEGO SPELT CRACKERS

Nutty Manchego cheese pairs perfectly with tangy sourdough in these better-than-store-bought cheese crackers. Using a biscuit cutter gives them a professional look and helps with a uniform bake. Spelt, an ancient variety of wheat, adds a sweet, nutty flavor to the cracker. You can find it in many supermarkets and health food stores and online.

MAKES 45 CRACKERS

60 g (½ cup) spelt flour

60 g (½ cup) all-purpose flour

3 g (½ tsp) coarse sea salt or Himalayan salt

½ tsp paprika

35 g (⅓ cup) grated Manchego cheese

75 g (5 tbsp) unsalted butter, cold, cut into pieces

226 g (1 cup) sourdough discard

14 g (1 tbsp) water

DAY 1

Preheat the oven to 400°F (200°C). Line an 18 x 13–inch (45 x 33–cm) baking sheet with parchment paper.

Whisk together the spelt flour, all-purpose flour, salt, paprika and Manchego cheese. Using a pastry cutter or two butter knives, incorporate the butter into the flour mixture until the mixture resembles coarse crumbs. Stir the sourdough discard and water into the mixture until they're fully incorporated. Gather the dough into a ball and squeeze it a few times to bring it together. Divide the dough in half.

Working with one portion at a time, place the dough between two pieces of parchment paper. Use a rolling pin to roll the dough out until it is ⅛ inch (3 mm) thick. With a 2-inch (5-cm) fluted biscuit cutter, cut as many crackers out of the dough as you can. Using a pastry scraper, transfer the dough disks onto the lined baking sheet. Repeat with the remaining dough and reroll the scraps. Fill the baking sheets and bake as many crackers as you can.

Bake the crackers for about 15 minutes, until they're a medium golden brown. Remove them from the oven and cool right on the pan.

When the crackers are cool, store them in an airtight container at room temperature for up to 1 month.

SEEDED FLATBREAD CRISPS

These crisps are the perfect topper for a cheese board—if you can stop yourself from devouring them all while you bake. A hint of pepper serves as the perfect complement to the tangy flavor of sourdough discard. The high proportion of pre-fermented flour makes these crackers easier to digest and a great healthy alternative to store-bought crackers.

MAKES APPROXIMATELY 30 CRACKERS

60 g (½ cup) all-purpose flour

28 g (2 tbsp) extra-virgin olive oil

3 g (½ tsp) ground black pepper

5 g (½ tbsp) poppy seeds

5 g (½ tbsp) sesame seeds

5 g (1 tsp) granulated sugar

5 g (1 tsp) sea salt

226 g (1 cup) sourdough discard

DAY 1

In a large bowl, combine the flour and olive oil, and rub to coat the flour with oil. Add the pepper, poppy seeds, sesame seeds, sugar and salt, and stir together. Stir the sourdough discard into the mixture until a shaggy dough begins to form. Press the dough together gently with your hands to form a ball and wrap the dough in plastic wrap. Let the dough rest for 30 minutes.

Preheat the oven to 450°F (230°C). Line a 9 x 13–inch (23 x 33–cm) baking sheet with parchment paper.

Divide the dough into four pieces. Roll out and bake each piece one at a time. On a lightly floured work surface, roll out the dough as thin as you can. If the dough starts to spring back, let it rest some more. The dough must be very thin. Once rolled, transfer it to the lined baking sheet.

Bake each flatbread for 10 minutes, flipping halfway through. Check on it periodically to ensure it is not browning too much.

Remove the flatbread from the oven and transfer it to a wire rack. Allow the flatbread to cool completely. Once cooled, break it into 2-inch (5-cm) crisps. You can store the crisps in an airtight container for up to 1 month.

SAGE-ONION GRISSINI

Grissini are thin, crispy Italian breadsticks. They're perfect for dipping into tomato sauces and soft cheeses. These are very simple to prepare and make a wonderful centerpiece set in a tall glass. The process starts with making a classic bread dough that only needs to rise once, so these can be prepared in one day.

MAKES 16 BREADSTICKS

56 g (¼ cup) active sourdough starter (see page 15)

150 g (⅔ cup) water

8 g (1½ tsp) coarse sea salt, plus more for sprinkling

180 g (1½ cups) bread flour

56 g (¼ cup) extra-virgin olive oil

¼ tsp onion powder

5 g (3 tsp) minced fresh sage

60 g (½ cup) semolina flour

DAY 1

In a large bowl, combine the sourdough starter, water, salt and bread flour. Stir the mixture together until it forms a well-incorporated, cohesive dough. Cover the bowl with plastic wrap and set aside for 1 hour.

Mix the olive oil, onion powder and sage into the dough. Fold the dough in the bowl for 10 minutes to fully incorporate the mix-ins and build structure into the wet dough. Cover the bowl with plastic wrap and set aside for 1 hour.

Do another set of folds in the mixing bowl, then transfer the dough into a rectangular airtight container (an 8-inch [20-cm] baking pan or a Pyrex dish covered with plastic wrap works in a pinch). Let the dough rise for 3 to 4 hours, or until it increases in volume by 30 percent and appears very bubbly.

Preheat your oven to 500°F (260°C). Line two 9 x 13–inch (23 x 33–cm) baking sheets with parchment paper.

Dust your work surface and the dough liberally with the semolina flour. Turn the dough out gently and use your hands to flatten it out into a 8 x 12–inch (20 x 30–cm) rectangle. Using a bench scraper or a large sharp knife, cut the dough into 16 slices, each about 8 inches (20 cm) long. Carefully pick up each piece and gently twist as you transfer it to the prepared baking sheet.

Sprinkle the sticks with more salt. Bake for 10 to 15 minutes, or until the breadsticks look evenly browned and crisp, not burned.

Remove the breadsticks from the oven, transfer to a wire rack and allow them to cool completely before serving. Store these breadsticks in an airtight container for up to 1 month.

SPELT AND EINKORN GRAHAM CRACKERS

Homemade graham crackers are not only more delicious than the store-bought kind, they are also free from chemicals and preservatives. These are made from hearty spelt and einkorn flours, ancient strains of flour that are said to be easier to digest. If you cannot find these flours, feel free to use whole wheat flour and all-purpose flour.

MAKES 12 CRACKERS

130 g (1 cup) spelt flour

60 g (½ cup) einkorn flour

4 g (1 tsp) baking powder

¼ tsp baking soda

⅛ tsp salt

57 g (4 tbsp) unsalted butter

62 g (¼ cup) brown sugar

56 g (¼ cup) sourdough discard

28 g (2 tbsp) whole milk

52 g (2½ tbsp) honey

7 g (1 tsp) vanilla extract

DAY 1

In a medium bowl, whisk together the spelt and einkorn flours, baking powder, baking soda and salt. Set aside.

In a large bowl, using a handheld electric mixer or a stand mixer, cream together the butter and sugar until they're light and fluffy, about 5 minutes. Add the flour mixture and mix until a soft dough forms, about 3 minutes. Fold in the sourdough discard, milk, honey and vanilla. The dough will feel soft and a little bit sticky. Turn it out onto a piece of plastic wrap and bring it together into a flat disk. Wrap the dough up and refrigerate it for at least 1 hour or overnight.

Preheat the oven to 325°F (160°C).

Divide the dough in half. Working with one portion at a time, place the dough between two pieces of parchment paper. Use a rolling pin to roll the dough out into a 10-inch (25-cm) square about 1⁄16 inch (1.5 mm) thick, trying to get the thickness as uniform as possible. Peel off the top piece of parchment. Using a pizza cutter or a sharp knife, trim the uneven edges of the dough. Score the dough into 3 x 4-inch (7.5 x 10-cm) rectangles, but do not separate them. Use a fork to prick holes in the top of the dough to prevent the crackers from puffing up in the oven. Transfer the sheet of dough, still on the parchment paper, to a baking sheet and bake for 15 minutes.

Take the baking sheet out of the oven and separate the crackers along the lines you scored in the dough. Bake the crackers for another 10 to 15 minutes, or until they are evenly browned and crisp.

Remove the crackers from the oven, transfer them to a wire rack and cool completely. Store the crackers in an airtight container at room temperature for up to 1 month.

BREAKFAST FAVORITES WITH A SOURDOUGH TWIST

You'll never go out for brunch again once you discover the simple pleasure of adding sourdough discard to all your breakfast favorites. The flavor of sourdough shines and adds complexity to Cream Cheese Biscuits (page 123) and Sourdough Crepes (page 119). The acidity of the discard has a tenderizing quality that results in the softest Blackberry-Ginger Scones (page 124) and the fluffiest Lemon-Ricotta Pancakes (page 120).

SOURDOUGH CREPES

Versatile and unfussy, you would never believe these delicate paper-thin crepes are so easy to make. Tender and a little bit tangy, these are the perfect blank canvas for both savory and sweet toppings and are sure to satisfy everyone's cravings.

MAKES 8 TO 10 CREPES

CREPES

90 g (¾ cup) all-purpose flour

4 g (½ tsp) kosher salt

4 g (1 tsp) granulated sugar

282 g (1¼ cups) whole milk

2 large eggs

113 g (½ cup) sourdough discard

57 g (4 tbsp) unsalted butter, melted, divided

SUGGESTED TOPPINGS

Fresh lemon juice

Sugar

Crème fraiche

Gruyère cheese

Black forest ham, thinly sliced

Fried eggs

DAY 1

In a large bowl, sift together the flour, salt and sugar. In a medium bowl, whisk together the milk, eggs and sourdough discard until fully combined. Add half the milk mixture to the flour and whisk until it's smooth. Whisk 28 grams (2 tablespoons) of the melted butter into the batter until it's fully incorporated. (You'll use the other half of the butter to cook the crepes.) Whisk in the remaining milk mixture until it's completely smooth.

At this point, the batter can be refrigerated for up to 2 days before cooking. It will separate, so simply stir it before moving on to the next step.

Heat a 12-inch (30-cm) nonstick skillet over medium-high heat for about 2 minutes. Brush the bottom of the skillet with melted butter and add ⅓ cup (80 ml) of batter to the center of the skillet. Being very careful, lift, tilt and rotate the skillet in a circular motion to evenly coat the bottom. Cook until the crepe is evenly golden, about 45 seconds, then flip and cook about 45 seconds on the other side. Using a rubber spatula, lift the edge of the crepe and slide it onto a plate. Place the cooked crepes in the oven on a very low setting (mine goes as low as 150°F [65°C]) to keep them warm while you cook the rest of the batter.

For sweet crepes, serve the warm crepes with a squeeze of lemon, a sprinkle of sugar and a dollop of crème fraiche.

For savory crepes, melt the Gruyère cheese in the center of the crepe after you flip it over. Slide the crepe onto a plate and add a layer of ham and a fried egg on top, then fold the edges of the crepe over the egg.

Keep any leftover, unfilled crepes refrigerated in a ziptop bag for up to 3 days. Reheat by frying the crepes in 5 grams (1 teaspoon) of butter for 30 seconds on each side.

LEMON-RICOTTA PANCAKES

I absolutely love pancakes for breakfast, but most recipes end up so dense that I can't have more than two or three bites. That's not the case with these tender, melt-in-your-mouth pancakes. With a bright tang from lemon and a soft, fluffy crumb thanks to the ricotta, you'll have to stop yourself from eating the whole stack.

MAKES 8 PANCAKES

113 g (½ cup) sourdough discard

28 g (2 tbsp) granulated sugar

88 g (½ cup) full-fat ricotta cheese

56 g (¼ cup) whole milk

1 large egg

Zest of 1 lemon

21 g (2 tbsp) fresh lemon juice

7 g (1 tsp) vanilla extract

60 g (½ cup) all-purpose flour

4 g (¾ tsp) baking soda

⅓ tsp baking powder

⅓ tsp kosher salt

Butter

SUGGESTED TOPPINGS

Maple syrup

Fresh berries

DAY 1

In a large bowl, mix the sourdough discard, sugar, ricotta, milk, egg, lemon zest, lemon juice and vanilla until they're combined. Sift the flour, baking soda, baking powder and salt into the bowl, and stir gently with a wooden spoon until only a few lumps remain. Avoid over-mixing the batter or your pancakes will turn out rubbery.

Heat a medium skillet over medium heat. Melt 14 grams (1 tablespoon) of butter on the skillet and wait for it to sizzle. Pour ¼ cup (60 ml) of the batter onto the skillet to make about a 5-inch (13-cm) pancake. Cook until it's golden brown, about 1 to 2 minutes on each side.

These pancakes are best served warm with maple syrup and fresh berries. Freeze leftover pancakes in a ziptop bag and toss them in the microwave for 40 seconds to reheat.

CREAM CHEESE BISCUITS

Wonderfully flaky with a tender crumb, these biscuits are the perfect addition to any brunch. Stacking the dough before rolling it out and then popping it in the freezer are the keys to achieving the heavenly layers in this homemade biscuit. Cream cheese helps further tenderize the crumb, and sourdough discard gives these biscuits a rich, complex flavor. These are a breeze to make and freeze beautifully, so you can enjoy a fresh-baked biscuit slathered in soft butter and jam even on the busiest of mornings.

MAKES 12 BISCUITS

56 g (4 tbsp) cream cheese

114 g (½ cup) unsalted butter

56 g (¼ cup) sourdough discard

170 g (¾ cup) whole milk

25 g (5 tsp) cornstarch

300 g (2½ cups) all-purpose flour

14 g (1 tbsp) granulated sugar

14 g (4 tsp) baking powder

4 g (½ tsp) salt

3 g (½ tsp) baking soda

180 g (¾ cup) cream

DAY 1

About 30 minutes to 1 hour before you are ready to bake, cut the cream cheese and butter into ½-inch (1.3-cm) pieces and put them in the freezer.

Place a rack in the middle of your oven and preheat it to 450°F (230°C). Line a 9 x 13–inch (23 x 33–cm) baking sheet with parchment paper.

In a large measuring cup, combine the sourdough discard and milk. Put it in the refrigerator until you're ready to use it.

In a large mixing bowl, whisk together the cornstarch, flour, sugar, baking powder, salt and baking soda until no lumps remain. Add the frozen cream cheese and butter pieces into the flour mixture, using a pastry blender to cut both into the flour until the mixture resembles coarse crumbs. Stir in the cold milk mixture. Your dough should look dry and shaggy.

Turn your dough out onto a work surface and knead briefly until the dough comes together. Roll the dough into an 8-inch (20-cm) square, cut it into four equal squares and stack the pieces. Using a rolling pin, flatten the stack into an 8 x 6–inch (80 x 15–cm) rectangle. Trim the edges and cut the dough into 12 squares of roughly the same size. Place the squares on your prepared baking sheet and freeze for 5 to 10 minutes.

Remove the pan from the freezer and brush the tops of the biscuits liberally with cream. Bake them until they are light brown, about 12 to 15 minutes. Transfer the biscuits to a wire rack and let them cool for 5 minutes. Serve warm, with a generous slathering of soft butter and jam.

Store unbaked biscuits by freezing them uncovered on a baking sheet for 2 hours and then transferring them into a ziptop bag. Do not thaw frozen biscuits before baking. Bake according to the directions above, but you may have to add 3 to 5 minutes to the baking time.

BLACKBERRY-GINGER SCONES

Fresh-baked scones are always a delightful revelation to anyone trying them for the first time. The addition of sourdough discard gives these scones a savory note that's enhanced by the freshness of ginger and sweet, tangy bursts of whole blackberries. Keep your ingredients cold for the best results; this will prevent your scones from spreading in the oven and guarantee you'll have tall scones with a nice, tender crumb.

MAKES 8 SCONES

113 g (½ cup) sourdough discard

1 large egg

150 g (⅔ cup) yogurt, sour cream or crème fraiche

75 g (⅓ cup) whole milk, plus more for brushing

50 g (¼ cup) granulated sugar

7 g (2 tsp) baking powder

2 g (½ tsp) baking soda

3 g (½ tsp) salt

4 g (2 tbsp) grated fresh ginger

300 g (2½ cups) all-purpose flour

114 g (½ cup) unsalted butter, cold, cut into pieces

130 g (1 cup) fresh blackberries

DAY 1

In a large measuring cup, stir together the sourdough discard, egg, yogurt and milk until everything is fully incorporated. Put the mixture in the refrigerator until you're ready to use it.

In a large bowl, whisk together the sugar, baking powder, baking soda, salt, ginger and flour. Add the butter and toss to coat. Using a pastry blender, cut the butter into the flour until only pea-sized pieces remain. Lightly toss the blackberries in the flour mixture. Form a well in the middle of the flour and pour the cold milk mixture into the center. Using a fork, incorporate the dry ingredients gradually, until a shaggy dough forms (it's okay if the dough appears dry). Lightly knead the dough in the bowl until it just comes together. Do not overwork or your scones will become tough.

Line a 9 x 13–inch (23 x 33–cm) baking sheet with parchment paper. Turn your dough out onto a lightly floured surface and pat it into a round disk about 1 inch (2.5 cm) thick. Cut the dough into eight wedges and place them on the lined baking sheet about 2 inches (5 cm) apart. Put the scones in the refrigerator for 30 minutes.

While your scones chill, preheat the oven to 375°F (190 °C).

Brush the tops of the scones with milk and bake until they're golden brown, about 25 to 30 minutes. Move them to a wire rack and cool slightly before serving. These scones are best enjoyed fresh but will keep well in an airtight container for up to 2 days.

COOKIE TOP BANANAS FOSTER MUFFINS

These muffins get their name from their characteristically crunchy top. While the top is the star of the show in most muffins, these are great from the bottom up, with an amazingly soft crumb that gets a flavor boost from the addition of sourdough starter and dark rum. Use whole milk in place of rum if you don't have any or just don't like rum. These treats have tall and wide muffin tops that spread, so you'll need to use two muffin pans, filling every other cavity, so the muffins do not stick to one another.

MAKES 9 MUFFINS

BATTER

284 g (1 cup) overripe bananas (about 2)

56 g (¼ cup) sourdough discard

28 g (2 tbsp) dark rum

227 g (1¾ cups) all-purpose flour, plus more for dusting

5 g (1 tsp) baking soda

3 g (¾ tsp) baking powder

9 g (1½ tsp) kosher salt

170 g (¾ cup) unsalted butter, softened

212 g (1 cup) brown sugar, plus more for dusting

2 large eggs, room temperature

150 g (½ cup) chopped pecans

28 g (2 tbsp) unsalted butter, melted

TOPPING

50 g (¼ cup) granulated sugar, plus more for dusting

3 g (1 tsp) ground cinnamon

¼ tsp ground nutmeg

DAY 1

In a medium bowl, mash the bananas using a wooden spoon. Stir in the sourdough discard and rum until they're fully combined. Set aside. In another medium bowl, whisk together the flour, baking soda, baking powder and salt. Set aside.

In a large bowl, using a handheld electric mixer, cream together the softened butter and brown sugar until it's light, fluffy and doubled in volume. Add the eggs one at a time, waiting until the first is fully incorporated before adding the other one. Add half the flour mixture to the creamed butter and mix until only a few streaks remain. Then add half the banana mixture, the rest of the flour mixture and the rest of the banana, mixing well between each addition. Stir in the pecans. Cover the bowl with plastic wrap and set aside to rest for 1 hour.

Preheat the oven to 400°F (200°C).

Prepare two 12-cup muffin pans by brushing every other cup with the melted butter; you'll fill six in one pan and three in the other. Dust the buttered slots with sugar and a little flour to prevent your muffins from sticking. Fill each prepared slot with 84 grams (6 tablespoons) of muffin batter. The muffin cups will seem overfilled—this is okay and will result in nice domed tops.

To make the topping, in a small bowl, mix together the sugar, cinnamon and nutmeg. Top each muffin liberally with this cinnamon sugar mixture.

Bake the muffins for 20 to 25 minutes, or until they are golden brown and a skewer inserted in the center comes out clean. Place the pans on a wire rack and allow the muffins to cool in the pans before turning them out. Do not try to remove the muffins from the pans before they are fully cool or they may collapse.

These muffins are best enjoyed warm. Store any leftovers in a ziptop bag at room temperature for up to 3 days.

LIÈGE WAFFLES

Not your ordinary diner waffle, these Liège waffles are in a class of their own. Basically brioche cooked in a waffle iron, these are sweet, dense and chewy inside, with a crispy crust and pockets of pearl sugar throughout. Using sourdough discard allows for a slow rise overnight; mix the dough up before bedtime and you can have hot, fresh waffles with your coffee in the morning. Crunchy pieces of pearl sugar throughout make these waffles special. You can get pearl sugar at specialty gourmet food stores or online. If you don't have any on hand, fruit or white chocolate chips will give a different effect but make for a delicious substitute.

MAKES 10 WAFFLES

70 g (⅓ cup) whole milk

75 g (⅓ cup) sourdough discard

1 large egg

25 g (⅛ cup) granulated sugar

7 g (½ tbsp) vanilla extract

240 g (2 cups) all-purpose flour

6 g (1 tsp) sea salt or kosher salt

140 g (10 tbsp) unsalted butter, softened

100 g (⅔ cup) pearl sugar

DAY 1

In a medium bowl, combine the milk, sourdough discard, egg, sugar and vanilla. Using your hand or a wooden spoon, stir until the sourdough has completely dissolved.

In a large bowl, whisk together the flour and salt. Pour the milk mixture into the flour and stir to combine, until the dough appears smooth. Add the butter to the dough 14 grams (1 tablespoon) at a time, and knead the dough in the bowl until each piece has been fully incorporated. Place the dough in a clean bowl and cover it with plastic wrap. Set aside and allow the dough to rest for 1 hour.

Knead the dough for 5 minutes, then perform one set of folds. Place the dough in an airtight container that gives it room to rise, and leave it to proof at room temperature overnight.

DAY 2

The next day, your dough should have increased in volume by at least 30 percent. Leaving the dough in the container, knead in the pearl sugar until it is evenly distributed throughout. Divide the dough into ten equal pieces and shape them into balls. Set the balls on your work surface, cover them with plastic wrap and allow them to rest for 30 minutes.

Preheat your waffle iron to a medium-high setting. I find that my nonstick waffle iron cooks these waffles perfectly well without greasing it, but if your waffle iron does not have a good nonstick coating, grease it with nonstick cooking spray or ghee.

Working with as many balls of dough as will fit in your iron, cook the waffles for 4 to 5 minutes. Enjoy them fresh off the iron topped with crème fraiche, Nutella, fruit or, my personal favorite, plain.

These cooked Liège waffles freeze beautifully for up to a month and can easily be heated up in a toaster. Cook up a double batch, and you'll have a crisp waffle any time you want.

EASY DECADENT CAKES

Scoring intricate designs on my sourdough loaves is my favorite part of baking bread, but I usually can't be bothered to top my cakes with fussy frostings or complicated decorations. My favorite cake recipes are ones with simple toppings or those that can stand on their own. The cakes in this chapter are uncomplicated and delicious. The tenderizing acidity of sourdough imparts a soft crumb, and the moisture locked in the discard helps keep cakes fresh and prevents them from going stale for longer than a typical cake.

GERMAN CHOCOLATE CAKE

My boyfriend is my creative baking muse—in large part because we live together, which forces me to incorporate sourdough into baked goods that he will love and, most importantly, eat. German chocolate is his favorite cake, which sent me on a quest to create the perfect sourdough discard chocolate cake. This batter is very thin and runny, but don't let that make you nervous; it's what gives the cake its light and airy texture.

MAKES 1 CAKE

CAKE BATTER

150 g (1¼ cups) all-purpose flour

300 g (1½ cups) granulated sugar

50 g (½ cup) unsweetened cocoa powder

2 g (½ tsp) baking soda

4 g (1 tsp) baking powder

4 g (½ tsp) kosher salt

170 g (¾ cup) strong brewed coffee

226 g (1 cup) whole milk

75 g (⅓ cup) vegetable oil

1 large egg

113 g (½ cup) sourdough discard

7 g (1 tsp) vanilla extract

COCONUT PECAN FROSTING

226 g (1 cup) whole milk

200 g (1 cup) granulated sugar

3 egg yolks

227 g (1 cup) unsalted butter

¼ tsp kosher salt

90 g (1 cup) sweetened coconut flakes

100 g (1 cup) chopped pecans

DAY 1

Preheat your oven to 350°F (160°C). Line a 9 x 13–inch (23 x 33–cm) baking pan with two large pieces of parchment paper, with overhang on all sides to form a sling.

In a large bowl, sift together the flour, sugar, cocoa, baking soda, baking powder and salt. In a medium bowl, combine the coffee, milk, oil, egg, sourdough discard and vanilla. Fold a little bit of the wet ingredients into the flour mixture with a wooden spoon.

With a stand mixer or a handheld electric mixer running on low speed, add the rest of the wet ingredients into the flour until they're fully incorporated, about 30 seconds to 1 minute.

Pour the batter into the prepared pan and bake for 35 to 40 minutes, until a toothpick inserted in the center comes out clean.

While the cake bakes, make the frosting. Combine the milk, sugar, egg yolks, butter and salt in a medium saucepan over medium heat. Stir continuously and cook until it's thickened, about 10 to 15 minutes. Remove the mixture from the heat and pour it through a fine sieve into a large bowl. Stir in the coconut and pecans.

Remove the cake from the oven and set the pan on a wire rack. Spread the frosting on top of the warm cake. Let it cool completely in the pan, then use the parchment paper sling to remove the cooled cake from the pan. Cut it into squares.

Store any leftover cake in an airtight container in the refrigerator for up to 1 week.

STREUSEL COFFEE CAKE

This is the quintessential coffee cake—crunchy cinnamon topping on a soft, rich butter cake. The flavor of sourdough discard works so well in this sugary sweet treat; plus, having the word "coffee" in its name means you can eat it for breakfast.

MAKES 1 CAKE

STREUSEL TOPPING

120 g (1 cup) mixed unsalted nuts

11 g (1 tbsp) cornstarch

25 g (3 tbsp) all-purpose flour

70 g (⅓ cup) brown sugar

42 g (3 tbsp) unsalted butter, cold, cut into pieces

CAKE

180 g (1½ cups) all-purpose flour

13 g (3 tsp) baking powder

7 g (1 tsp) kosher salt

114 g (½ cup) unsalted butter, softened

200 g (1 cup) granulated sugar

113 g (½ cup) sourdough discard

1 large egg

175 g (¾ cup) whole milk

DAY 1

Preheat the oven to 350°F (175°C). Line an 8-inch (20-cm) square cake pan with a large piece of parchment paper, with overhang on all sides to form a sling.

To make the streusel topping, divide the nuts in half. Chop half into large pieces and set them aside to use as a topping later. Finely chop the other half, place them in a small bowl and add the cornstarch, flour, brown sugar and butter. Mix everything with your hands until the mixture resembles coarse crumbs. Set aside.

To make the cake, in a large bowl, mix together the flour, baking powder, salt, butter, sugar, sourdough discard, egg and milk until they're blended and only a few streaks of flour remain. Be careful not to over-mix or your cake will turn out tough. Spread half the batter in the pan, sprinkle half the streusel over the batter and top with the remaining batter.

Bake the cake for 20 minutes. Remove it from the oven and top with the remaining streusel mix, spreading more streusel toward the edges so the middle of the cake doesn't sink. Sprinkle the reserved large pieces of nuts evenly over the cake, return it to the oven and bake for another 10 to 15 minutes, or until it's golden brown and a toothpick inserted in the center comes out clean.

Let the coffee cake cool for about 10 minutes in the pan, then remove it using the paper sling and transfer it to a wire rack. This cake is best enjoyed warm with a cup of coffee. Store any leftover cake in an airtight container at room temperature. The cake will stay tender for 1 week.

ALMOND-ORANGE OLIVE OIL CAKE

Top-quality olive oil imparts a rich flavor and an incredibly moist and tender crumb to this Mediterranean classic. Delicate orange zest and hints of nutty almond extract add such a nuanced flavor to this cake that you won't miss frosting at all.

MAKES 1 CAKE

120 g (1 cup) all-purpose flour

60 g (½ cup) ground almonds

5 g (¾ tsp) baking powder

6 g (¾ tsp) kosher salt

56 g (¼ cup) freshly squeezed orange juice

56 g (¼ cup) whole milk

¼ tsp almond extract

113 g (½ cup) sourdough discard

3 large eggs

240 g (1¼ cups) granulated sugar

Zest of 1 orange

177 g (¾ cup) extra-virgin olive oil

Powdered sugar, to dust (optional)

DAY 1

Adjust the oven rack to the middle position and preheat your oven to 350°F (175°C). Grease a 10-inch (25-cm) round springform pan.

In a medium bowl, whisk together the flour, ground almonds, baking powder and salt. In a small bowl, combine the orange juice, milk, almond extract and sourdough discard, and stir until they're well combined. Set both aside.

In a large bowl, using a stand mixer with a whisk attachment or a handheld electric mixer, whip the eggs on medium speed until they're foamy, about 1 minute. Add the sugar and orange zest, increase the speed to high and whip until the mixture is fluffy and pale yellow, about 5 minutes. Lower the speed to medium and, with the mixer running, slowly pour in the oil. Mix until the oil is fully incorporated, about 1 minute.

Add half the flour mixture and mix on low speed until it's incorporated, about 1 minute, scraping down the bowl as needed. Add the sourdough mixture and mix until everything is combined, about 30 seconds. Add the remaining flour mixture and mix until it's just incorporated, about 1 minute, scraping down the bowl as needed.

Transfer the batter to the prepared springform pan. Bake until the cake is deep golden brown and a toothpick inserted in the center comes out with only a few crumbs attached, about 40 to 45 minutes.

Transfer the pan to a wire rack and allow the cake to cool for 15 minutes. Remove the side of the pan and let the cake cool completely, about 1½ hours. Dust it with powdered sugar, if desired, cut into wedges and serve. Store any leftovers in an airtight container at room temperature for up to 1 week.

PIÑA COLADA UPSIDE DOWN CAKE

This retro cake is a favorite in our household. It's a perfect buttery cake baked on top of a sticky coconut butterscotch filling. You make the topping first in this recipe because it goes on the bottom. If you're using canned pineapple rings, make sure to drain them well and pat them dry.

MAKES 1 CAKE

COCONUT BUTTERSCOTCH FILLING

28 g (2 tbsp) unsalted butter

120 g (½ cup) coconut milk

200 g (1 cup) brown sugar

¼ tsp salt

26 g (2 tbsp) dark rum (optional)

7 pineapple rings

7 maraschino cherries

BATTER

150 g (1¼ cups) all-purpose flour

6 g (1½ tsp) baking powder

5 g (¾ tsp) salt

1 large egg

2 egg whites

114 g (½ cup) unsalted butter

171 g (¾ cup) granulated sugar

80 g (⅓ cup) sourdough discard

50 g (¼ cup) coconut milk

40 g (½ cup) sweetened coconut flakes

DAY 1

To make the filling, melt the butter in a saucepan over medium heat. Then add the coconut milk, brown sugar and salt. Stir until the sugar has melted. Without stirring, let the mixture come to a bubbling simmer for 2½ minutes. Remove the pan from the heat and cool for 5 minutes, then pour in the rum, if desired, and stir.

Pour the butterscotch filling into a 9-inch (23-cm) round cake pan. Arrange the pineapple rings and maraschino cherries on top of the filling and set it aside while you make the cake batter.

Preheat the oven to 350°F (175°C).

To make the batter, in a medium bowl, whisk together the flour, baking powder and salt. Set aside.

Put the egg and egg whites in a small bowl. Using a handheld electric mixer, whip the eggs until they're frothy and aerated, about 2 to 3 minutes. Set aside.

In a large bowl, cream the butter and sugar until the mixture appears light and fluffy. Add the whipped eggs and sourdough discard to your creamed butter. Then add one-third of the flour mixture to the butter mixture and stir using a spatula until just combined. Now add the coconut milk and stir. Stir in the remaining flour and gently fold in the coconut flakes. Your batter should be very thick.

Carefully spoon the cake batter into the cake pan, being careful not to disturb your design on the bottom. Gently smooth out the top of your cake. Place the cake pan on a cookie sheet and bake for 50 to 60 minutes, until the cake is golden brown and a toothpick inserted in the middle comes out clean.

Cool for 10 minutes on a wire rack, then place a serving plate over the cake pan. Invert the cake pan and plate together and lift off the cake pan to release the cake. Allow the cake to cool for about 30 minutes, then cut it into pieces and serve.

This cake can be enjoyed warm or at room temperature. Store any leftover cake covered in the refrigerator for 2 to 3 days.

LEMON-BLUEBERRY POUND CAKE

Traditionally made with a pound of flour, eggs, sugar and butter, adding moisture from sourdough makes this version of pound cake lighter. Adding oil along with the butter results in a flavorful, rich cake with a more tender, softer crumb. Aromatic lemon zest and bursts of whole blueberries create a delicious cake that makes a perfect dessert.

MAKES 1 CAKE

150 g (1 cup) fresh blueberries

127 g (1 cup + 1 tbsp) all-purpose flour, divided

30 g (¼ cup) cornstarch

5 g (1 tsp) baking powder

4 g (½ tsp) salt

150 g (⅔ cup) unsalted butter, divided

75 g (⅓ cup) grapeseed oil (or any neutral-flavored oil)

277 g (1¼ cups) granulated sugar

4 g (2 tsp) lemon zest

18 g (2 tbsp) fresh lemon juice

4 large eggs

5 g (1½ tsp) vanilla extract

56 g (¼ cup) sourdough discard

DAY 1

Put a rack at the middle position in your oven and preheat the oven to 325°F (160°C). Line an 8 x 4-inch (20 x 10-cm) loaf pan with parchment paper.

In a small bowl, toss the blueberries with 7 grams (1 tablespoon) of flour to coat, and set aside. In a medium bowl, whisk together the remaining 120 grams (1 cup) of flour, cornstarch, baking powder and salt until no lumps remain, and set aside.

Melt 113 grams (½ cup) of butter in a small saucepan over medium heat. Turn off the heat and whisk in the oil and remaining butter until the butter is melted and everything is fully incorporated.

In a food processor or blender, pulse the sugar, lemon zest, lemon juice, eggs and vanilla until they're well combined. Keep the processor running and add the butter and oil in a steady stream until the mixture has emulsified, about 20 seconds.

Transfer the mixture to a large bowl and fold in the sourdough discard. Sift the flour mixture over the egg mixture one-third at a time, whisking gently after each addition until just combined. Fold in the blueberries, being careful not to over-mix.

Pour the batter into the prepared pan. Bake the loaf for 50 to 60 minutes, or until it's golden brown and a toothpick inserted in the center comes out clean.

Allow your lemon pound cake to cool in the pan for 10 minutes, then turn it out onto a wire rack. Allow to cool for at least 1 hour before serving. The cake will keep stored in a ziptop bag at room temperature for up to 3 days.

ZUCCHINI BREAD

Zucchini makes an incredibly moist and flavorful loaf cake, combined with aromatic cinnamon and hearty walnuts. Using vegetable oil instead of butter creates a light, tender crumb, and the addition of sourdough keeps these loaves from going stale for days.

MAKES 2 LOAVES

270 g (2 cups) grated zucchini

345 g (2¾ cups) all-purpose flour

6 g (1 tsp) kosher salt

8 g (3 tsp) ground cinnamon

1.5 g (¼ tsp) baking powder

5 g (1 tsp) baking soda

3 large eggs

143 g (¾ cup) vegetable oil

5 g (1 tsp) vanilla extract

420 g (2 cups) granulated sugar

113 g (½ cup) sourdough discard

65 g (½ cup) chopped walnuts

DAY 1

Preheat your oven to 325°F (160°C). Line two 8 x 4–inch (20 x 10–cm) loaf pans with parchment paper.

Place the grated zucchini in a sieve over a bowl and press it with the back of a spoon to remove some moisture. Set aside to drain.

In a medium bowl, whisk together the flour, salt, cinnamon, baking powder and baking soda until no clumps remain. Set aside.

In a large bowl, beat together the eggs, oil, vanilla and sugar until the mixture appears light and has increased slightly in volume. Fold the sourdough discard into the egg mixture. Add the flour mixture and mix until only a few streaks of flour remain. Stir in the zucchini and walnuts until well combined. Pour the batter into the loaf pans.

Bake for 50 to 60 minutes, or until a toothpick inserted in the center of each loaf comes out clean. Set the pans on a wire rack and cool the loaves in the pans for 20 minutes. Remove the loaves from the pans and allow to cool completely before slicing.

Store the loaves in a ziptop bag at room temperature for up to 3 days.

IRRESISTIBLE COOKIES AND BROWNIES

Cookies were the first baked items I made with my sourdough discard, so the recipes in this chapter are very close to my heart. Sourdough discard, along with spices, nuts, zests and floral notes, tames the sugary sweetness of these cookies. It also adds moisture that helps the cookies remain fresh for a longer time. I love reinventing classic cookie recipes by adding aromatic ingredients, as in my Orange-Chocolate Chunk Cookies (page 147) and Rosewater-Cardamom-Pistachio Biscotti (page 152).

ORANGE-CHOCOLATE CHUNK COOKIES

Orange zest is a fragrant addition and the perfect complement to classic chocolate chip cookies. Melting the butter, adding the perfect proportion of sourdough discard and shaping the cookie dough into larger portions ensure these cookies maintain their delicious chewy texture. Melt the butter in a lighter-colored saucepan so you can carefully monitor the color change.

MAKES 16 LARGE COOKIES

170 g (¾ cup) unsalted butter

240 g (2 cups) all-purpose flour

3 g (½ tsp) baking soda

7 g (1 tsp) salt

172 g (¾ cup) brown sugar

100 g (½ cup) granulated sugar

12 g (4 tsp) orange zest (from 2 oranges)

6 g (2 tsp) vanilla extract

2 egg yolks

113 g (½ cup) sourdough discard

166 g (1 cup) chocolate chunks

DAY 1

In a small saucepan, melt the butter over medium heat. Swirl the pan occasionally to be sure the butter is cooking evenly. As the butter melts, the color will progress from lemony yellow to golden tan to, finally, a toasty brown. Once the butter smells nutty and is the color of graham cracker crumbs, take the pan off the heat and pour the butter into a large heatproof bowl. Set aside and let the butter cool slightly.

Preheat your oven to 375°F (190°C). Line a large baking sheet with parchment paper.

In a medium bowl, whisk together the flour, baking soda and salt. Set aside.

Add the brown sugar, granulated sugar, orange zest and vanilla to the butter, and mix with a spatula until the sugars have melted. Set aside and let the mixture stand for about 5 minutes. Then add the egg yolks and sourdough discard, and stir until everything is fully incorporated. Slowly add in the flour mixture a little bit at a time. Finally, add the chocolate chunks and mix until no flour pockets remain.

Scoop out the cookie dough in 30- to 42-gram (2- to 3-tablespoon) portions. Place the cookies on the lined baking sheet 2 inches (5 cm) apart. Bake for 10 to 14 minutes, or until the edges have set but the centers are still soft. Be careful not to over-bake or the cookies will lose their chewy texture. They should look slightly wet on top with browned bottoms.

Remove from the oven. Cool the cookies on the sheet for 5 minutes to fully set. Transfer the cookies to a wire rack and allow them to fully cool before serving. Store these cookies in an airtight container for up to 2 weeks.

WHITE CHOCOLATE-CRANBERRY OATMEAL COOKIES

Oatmeal cookies were the first baked goods I ever made. I still remember the mind-blowing pleasure of biting into a warm cookie fresh from the oven for the first time. Sweet white chocolate chips and tangy cranberries are the perfect complement to the savory notes sourdough discard brings to these cookies.

MAKES 20 LARGE COOKIES

90 g (¾ cup) all-purpose flour

5 g (1 tsp) coarse sea salt or Himalayan salt

4 g (½ tsp) baking soda

57 g (4 tbsp) unsalted butter

¼ tsp ground cinnamon

175 g (¾ cup) brown sugar

100 g (½ cup) granulated sugar

109 g (½ cup) vegetable oil

56 g (¼ cup) sourdough discard

1 large egg

1 egg yolk

6 g (1 tsp) vanilla extract

300 g (2¼ cups) quick oats

100 g (¾ cup) dried cranberries

100 g (½ cup) white chocolate chips

DAY 1

Preheat your oven to 375°F (190°C). Line two large rimmed baking sheets with parchment paper.

In a medium bowl, whisk together the flour, salt and baking soda. Set aside.

Add the butter to a small saucepan over medium-high heat and cook until it browns, swirling the pan occasionally, until the foaming subsides. Stir and scrape the bottom of the pan with a heat-resistant spatula until the milk solids are dark golden brown and the butter has a nutty aroma, 1 to 2 minutes. Immediately pour it into a large heatproof bowl. Stir in the cinnamon. Add the brown sugar, granulated sugar, oil and sourdough discard to the bowl, and whisk until everything is combined. Add the egg, egg yolk and vanilla, and whisk until the mixture is smooth.

Using a wooden spoon or spatula, stir in the flour mixture until everything is fully combined, about 1 minute. Mix in the oats, cranberries and chocolate chips, and stir until they're evenly distributed.

Scoop out 30- to 42-gram (2- to 3-tablespoon) portions of the cookie dough and arrange the dough balls 2 inches (5 cm) apart on the lined sheets. Use your hand to gently press the top of each ball to flatten it a bit. Bake, one sheet at a time, until the cookie edges are set and lightly browned and the centers are still soft but not wet, 8 to 10 minutes.

Let the cookies cool and set on the sheet for 10 minutes. Use a wide metal spatula to transfer the cookies to a wire rack and let them cool completely. Store the cookies in a ziptop bag at room temperature for up to 3 days.

HAZELNUT SANDIES

Buttery, nutty sandies are my favorite type of cookie. To achieve their characteristically crumbly texture, the dough needs to have a relatively low hydration, so adding sourdough starter can be a bit tricky. After testing, I came up with the perfect formula that results in a delicate cookie that's not greasy and will not fall apart.

MAKES 16 COOKIES

190 g (1½ cups) shelled hazelnuts

113 g (½ cup) packed brown sugar

26 g (¼ cup) confectioners' sugar

210 g (1¾ cups) all-purpose flour

4 g (½ tsp) kosher salt

28 g (2 tbsp) vegetable oil

114 g (½ cup) unsalted butter, cold, cut into pieces

1 egg yolk

56 g (¼ cup) sourdough discard

DAY 1

Preheat the oven to 350°F (175°C).

Spread the hazelnuts in a single layer on a large baking sheet and toast for 5 to 10 minutes. Set aside to cool.

When the nuts are cool, combine the toasted hazelnuts, brown sugar and confectioners' sugar in the bowl of a food processor, and pulse until the nuts are finely ground. Add the flour, salt, oil and butter, and process to combine until the mixture resembles wet sand. Finally, add the egg yolk and sourdough discard, and process until combined.

Divide the dough in half and place each portion on a piece of parchment paper. Use your hands to roll each piece into a log about 2 inches (5 cm) in diameter and roll it up in the paper. Twist the ends of the parchment paper to seal. Chill the dough for 2 hours.

Adjust the racks on your oven to the upper and lower middle positions. Preheat the oven to 325°F (162°C). Line two large baking sheets with parchment paper.

Working with one log at a time, unwrap the dough and use a sharp knife to cut it into ⅜-inch (9-mm) slices. Place the cookies ½ inch (13 cm) apart on the cookie sheet (they won't spread too much). Bake for 10 minutes with one cookie sheet on the top rack and another in the middle. Switch the cookie sheets and bake for another 10 to 15 minutes, or until the cookies are browned and crisp.

Allow the cookies to cool for 5 minutes on the baking sheet, then transfer them to a wire rack to cool completely. These are best enjoyed fully cooled and can be stored in an airtight container at room temperature for up to 1 month.

ROSEWATER-CARDAMOM-PISTACHIO BISCOTTI

Turkish-inspired flavors give these classic crisp Italian cookies a very different twist. The water locked in your sourdough helps these cookies stay fresh and not go stale.

MAKES 32 BISCOTTI

DOUGH

140 g (1¼ cups) shelled unsalted pistachios, divided

240 g (2 cups) all-purpose flour

8 g (2 tsp) baking powder

3 g (1 tsp) ground cardamom

¼ tsp kosher salt

2 large eggs

200 g (1 cup) granulated sugar

57 g (4 tbsp) unsalted butter, melted and cooled

56 g (¼ cup) sourdough discard

21 g (1½ tsp) rosewater

2 g (½ tsp) vanilla extract

EGG WASH

1 egg white

Pinch of salt

DAY 1

Adjust your oven rack to the middle position. Preheat the oven to 325°F (160°C). Line an 18 x 13-inch (46 x 33-cm) baking sheet with parchment paper.

Coarsely chop 112 grams (1 cup) of pistachios and set aside. Grind the remaining 28 grams (¼ cup) of pistachios in a food processor until they're finely ground, about 45 seconds. Transfer the ground nuts to a medium mixing bowl and whisk in the flour, baking powder, cardamom and salt.

In the food processor, add the eggs and pulse until they've lightened in color and almost doubled in volume, about 2 minutes. While the food processor is running, slowly add the sugar until it's fully incorporated, about 15 seconds. Add the butter, sourdough discard, rosewater and vanilla, and process until everything is combined, about 10 seconds.

Transfer the egg mixture to a large bowl. Fold half of the nut and flour mixture into the egg mixture and, using a spatula, gently fold until it's just combined. Add the remaining flour mixture, then gently fold in the chopped pistachios until they're fully combined.

Transfer the dough to your lined baking sheet. Using floured hands, form two 8 x 3-inch (20 x 7-cm) rectangles spaced 4 inches (10 cm) apart on the baking sheet. They will be quite thick. Spray a spatula with nonstick cooking spray and gently smooth the tops and sides of the loaves.

To make the egg wash, in a small bowl, whisk together the egg white and salt. Brush the tops of the loaves with the egg wash. Bake until the loaves are golden and just beginning to crack on top, about 30 to 35 minutes.

Let the loaves cool on the baking sheet for 30 minutes, then transfer them to a cutting board. Using a serrated knife, cut ½-inch (1.3-cm) slices. Lay the slices, cut side down, on the baking sheet and bake again for 17 minutes. Flip and continue baking for another 17 minutes, until the biscotti are crisp and golden brown on both sides.

Cool the biscotti completely on a wire rack before serving. Biscotti can be stored in an airtight container at room temperature for up to 1 month.

BUTTERSCOTCH FUDGE BROWNIES

Chocolate lovers will adore this recipe. With its intense chocolate flavor, these brownies are not for the faint of heart, though. This recipe begins with a basic butterscotch sauce, which gives the brownies a very fudgy texture with no cakiness. Sourdough adds a slight tang that helps cut through the bitterness of the baker's chocolate. Go for semi-sweet instead of unsweetened chocolate if you're more of a milk chocolate fan.

MAKES 16 BROWNIES

57 g (4 tbsp) unsalted butter

75 g (⅓ cup) brown sugar

56 g (¼ cup) unsweetened baker's chocolate

2 large eggs

7 g (1 tsp) salt

113 g (½ cup) sourdough discard

85 g (⅔ cup) all-purpose flour

28 g (¼ cup) cocoa powder

7 g (1 tsp) vanilla extract

145 g (⅔ cup) granulated sugar

28 g (2 tbsp) vegetable oil

DAY 1

Preheat your oven to 325°F (160°C). Line an 8 x 8-inch (20 x 20-cm) baking pan with parchment paper.

In a small saucepan over medium heat, melt the butter, brown sugar and chocolate, stirring to combine. When everything is melted and combined, transfer the mixture to a large mixing bowl and allow it to cool slightly. Gently stir in the eggs, salt, sourdough discard, flour, cocoa powder, vanilla, sugar and oil until only a few lumps remain.

Pour the batter into your prepared baking pan and bake for 20 to 25 minutes, or until the center of the brownies has just set.

Allow the brownies to cool in the pan for 15 minutes before slicing. Store any leftover brownies in an airtight container at room temperature for up to 3 days.

BUTTERY, FLAKY SOURDOUGH PASTRIES AND TARTS

Pastry dough was the most difficult for me to master, perhaps because pastry-making techniques are so different from breadmaking. Heat, excessive moisture and gluten development are enemies of flaky, buttery crusts, so keeping your dough cool and using precise hydration and a gentle hand are key. Overcoming these challenges makes mastering pastry all the more fulfilling. However, just as with breadmaking, perfecting pastry takes practice.

In testing and experimenting with different methods, I was able to create buttery, flaky baked goods that benefit from the unique flavor of sourdough. Adding sourdough imparts a delicious, savory, cheesy quality to pastry that's a beautiful complement to savory or sweet fillings. The recipes in this chapter are simple to make and don't require blind baking or complicated shaping, like my elegant but simple Mixed Berry Galette (page 159) and the rustic classic Apricot Dumpling Cobbler (page 165). You'll even find savory Moroccan-Inspired Chicken Empanadas (page 166).

MIXED BERRY GALETTE

Unfussy and rustic, a galette is a free-form crusty cake with fruit inside. It's an elegant alternative to pie. A little bit of whole wheat adds nuttiness to the buttery crust. To avoid a soggy bottom, spread a layer of cookie crumbs on the bottom of your unbaked crust—crushed Spelt and Einkorn Graham Crackers (page 115) work perfectly.

MAKES 1 GALETTE

CRUST

80 g (⅔ cup) all-purpose flour

40 g (⅓ cup) whole wheat flour

3 g (½ tsp) kosher salt

114 g (½ cup) butter

113 g (½ cup) sourdough discard

28 g (2 tbsp) ice water

FILLING

160 g (1⅓ cups) fresh blueberries

160 g (1⅓ cups) fresh blackberries

60 g (⅓ cup) fresh raspberries

10 g (2 tsp) cornstarch

5 g (¾ tsp) kosher salt

66 g (⅓ cup) granulated sugar

5 g (1 tsp) vanilla extract

1 egg white, beaten

40 g (⅓ cup) cookie crumbs

DAY 1

To make the crust, in a medium bowl, whisk together the all-purpose flour, whole wheat flour and salt. Rub the butter into the flour, flattening the pieces into the size of walnut halves (larger pieces make for a flakier crust). Stir in the sourdough discard. Then add the water 14 grams (1 tablespoon) at a time, just until the dough comes together. Don't add too much, or the pastry will become too tough, but you can add a little more if necessary. When the dough comes together into a ball, wrap it in plastic wrap and refrigerate for at least 2 hours.

Line an 18 x 13–inch (45 x 33–cm) baking sheet with parchment paper.

Lightly flour your work surface and roll the dough out into a 12-inch (30-cm) circle. Roll in one direction, and turn the dough 90 degrees after each roll. This will keep the dough from sticking and maintain a uniform thickness. Place the dough on the prepared baking sheet and refrigerate while you make the filling.

To make the filling, in a large bowl, toss the blueberries, blackberries and raspberries with the cornstarch, salt, sugar and vanilla, and set aside for 2 to 3 minutes so the flavors can blend.

Take the crust out of the refrigerator. Brush the inside bottom of the crust with egg white and coat evenly with cookie crumbs. Spoon the filling into the middle of the dough, leaving a 2-inch (5-cm) border. Fold the crust up and over the fruit around the edges, pinching to seal it where it overlaps. Refrigerate the galette for 30 minutes.

(Continued)

EGG WASH

1 egg white

Pinch of salt

TOPPING

28 g (2 tbsp) turbinado sugar

42 g (3 tbsp) unsalted butter, cut in small pieces

Preheat the oven to 400°F (200°C).

To make the egg wash, whisk the egg white and salt in a small bowl. Brush the crust with egg wash.

To make the topping, sprinkle turbinado sugar on the crust and place the pieces of butter on the filling. Bake for 35 to 40 minutes, or until the crust is evenly browned.

Cool the galette for 15 minutes on the baking sheet, then transfer it to a wire rack to cool slightly before serving. Refrigerate leftover galette in an airtight container for up to 3 days.

PEAR-PISTACHIO FRANGIPANE TARTS

These tarts would be welcome in any pastry case. My cheater's puff pastry uses grated frozen butter instead of a butter block, which allows the dough to come together quicker and with less hassle. There's nothing quite like seeing puff pastry rise in the oven. For the best chances of success, keep your dough cold to prevent the butter from melting.

MAKES 6 TARTS

CHEATER'S PUFF PASTRY

240 g (2 cups) all-purpose flour

5 g (¾ tsp) kosher salt

227 g (1 cup) unsalted butter, frozen in 2 sticks, divided

113 g (½ cup) sourdough discard

28 g (2 tbsp) ice water

DAY 1

To make the pastry, in a medium bowl, mix the flour and salt. Coat both sticks of butter in the flour, then cut 57 grams (4 tablespoons) of butter into ½-inch (1.3-cm) pieces and add it to the flour. Return the rest of the butter to the freezer. Using your fingertips, rub in the butter pieces until the flour mixture resembles breadcrumbs. Stir in the sourdough discard, then add the water 14 grams (1 tablespoon) at a time to form a dough. Flatten the dough out into a rough square, wrap it in plastic wrap and refrigerate for 30 minutes.

While the pastry dough chills, grate the remaining frozen butter on a box grater and return it to the freezer.

Dust your work surface with flour and roll the dough out into a 12 x 4–inch (30 x 10–cm) rectangle. Spread the grated butter on the bottom third of the dough. Fold into thirds toward the center, as if you're folding a letter. Pinch the edges to seal. Turn the dough 90 degrees and roll the dough out into a 12 x 4–inch (30 x 10–cm) rectangle again. Fold the dough into thirds, wrap it in plastic wrap and return it to the refrigerator for another 30-minute rest. Repeat rolling and folding three or four more times. More folds result in more flaky layers, but be careful not to over-work the dough or the butter may be absorbed and you'll end up with shortcrust instead of puff pastry. You want to see plenty of dough and butter layers when you cut a cross section. Chill the pastry dough overnight.

(Continued)

PISTACHIO FRANGIPANE

56 g (½ cup) shelled unsalted pistachios

50 g (¼ cup) granulated sugar

1 large egg

14 g (1 tbsp) unsalted butter

4 g (1 tsp) vanilla extract

TOPPING

2 pears

14 g (1 tbsp) apricot preserves

DAY 2

To make the pistachio frangipane, in a food processor, process the pistachios, sugar, egg, butter and vanilla until a paste forms. Place the frangipane in an airtight container and refrigerate until you're ready to assemble your tarts.

Preheat your oven to 425°F (220°C). Line an 18 x 13–inch (45 x 33–cm) baking sheet with parchment paper.

On a lightly floured surface, roll the dough out into a 10 x 15–inch (25 x 38–cm) rectangle. Trim the edges of the rectangle and cut it into six 4-inch (10-cm) squares. Place them on the baking sheet 2 inches (5 cm) apart. Spread 14 grams (1 tablespoon) of frangipane on each piece of dough. Put the baking sheet in the refrigerator and chill for 15 minutes.

While it's chilling, quarter and core the pears. Slice each pear quarter lengthwise into four or five slices, starting at the rounded bottom, but try to keep them connected at the top. Using the palm of your hand, gently flatten and fan out the slices. Place the fanned pear quarters on top of the chilled tart pastry—you'll end up with more pears than you need.

Bake the tarts for 15 to 20 minutes, or until the pastry is golden brown and the frangipane is crusty. Remove from the oven. Microwave the apricot preserves for 30 seconds and brush it on top of the warm tarts.

Transfer the tarts to a wire rack to cool before serving. These are best enjoyed freshly baked but can be stored in an airtight container at room temperature for up to 3 days.

APRICOT DUMPLING COBBLER

In this recipe, I forego popular cobbler toppings and instead opt for an all-butter pastry. Leftover dough is baked in the middle, resulting in a steamed, buttery dumpling layer. Although I use apricots, bake with what's in season, like peaches in summer or plums in fall. Good quality canned peaches work too!

MAKES 1 COBBLER

CRUST

120 g (1 cup) all-purpose flour

7 g (1 tsp) kosher salt

14 g (1 tbsp) granulated sugar

227 g (1 cup) unsalted butter, frozen

56 g (½ cup) sourdough discard

56 g (¼ cup) ice water

FILLING

226 g (1 cup) water

8 g (1 tbsp) cornstarch

¼ tsp ground cinnamon

⅛ tsp ground nutmeg

165 g (¾ cup) granulated sugar

1 kg (6 cups) apricots, pitted and quartered

14 g (1 tbsp) unsalted butter

4 g (1 tsp) vanilla extract

¼ tsp almond extract

14 g (1 tbsp) orange liqueur (optional)

TOPPING

57 g (4 tbsp) unsalted butter, melted

28 g (2 tbsp) turbinado sugar

DAY 1

To make the crust, in a medium bowl, whisk together the flour, salt and sugar until no lumps remain. Rub the butter into the flour, flattening the pieces into the size of walnut halves.

Stir in the sourdough discard. Then add the water a few tablespoons at a time and mix just until the dough comes together. When the mixture clumps together into a ball, flatten it into a disk, wrap the dough in plastic wrap and refrigerate for at least 2 hours or overnight.

To make the filling, in a large saucepan over medium heat, combine the water, cornstarch, cinnamon, nutmeg and sugar. Cook until the mixture is thickened, about 3 minutes. Add the apricots and butter, and stir gently until the fruit is heated through, about 5 minutes. Remove from the heat and stir in the vanilla, almond extract and orange liqueur, if using. Set aside to cool to room temperature.

Preheat your oven to 425°F (220°C). Spoon half of the apricot filling into an 8-inch (20-cm) round baking dish. Set aside.

On a lightly floured surface, roll out your crust to about ⅛ inch (3 mm) thick. Using a 2-inch (5-cm) round biscuit cutter, cut out 26 rounds. You should have dough left over. Layer the leftover dough over the apricot filling and top that with the remaining filling. Place the dough rounds in a decorative pattern on top of your cobbler. For the topping, pour the melted butter on top of the cobbler and sprinkle with turbinado sugar.

Bake for 40 to 50 minutes, or until the fruit is bubbly and the crust appears golden brown. Cool completely, about 30 minutes, before serving.

Enjoy warm with a dollop of fresh whipped cream. Store any leftover cobbler in an airtight container in the refrigerator for up to 3 days.

MOROCCAN-INSPIRED CHICKEN EMPANADAS

Sourdough lends a delicious, almost cheesy flavor to buttery crust, making it the perfect accompaniment to savory pastries such as these empanadas. They're inspired by Moroccan bastilla, which traditionally feature a spiced chicken filling and a sweet cinnamon topping. I substitute heartier shortcrust enriched with eggs, lard and butter, instead of the traditional *warqa*—a thin Moroccan pastry.

MAKES 10 TO 15 EMPANADAS

CRUST

240 g (2 cups) all-purpose flour

4 g (½ tsp) salt

56 g (4 tbsp) lard

57 g (4 tbsp) unsalted butter, cold

4 g (½ tsp) fresh lemon juice

1 large egg

56 g (¼ cup) sourdough discard

42 g (3 tbsp) ice water

FILLING

2 g (1 tsp) ground ginger

4 g (1 tsp) ground cinnamon

2 g (½ tsp) ground turmeric

381 g (1 large) boneless skinless chicken breast

15 g (1 tbsp) olive oil

127 g (1 cup) diced white onion

56 g (¼ cup) chicken stock

12 g (3 tsp) fresh lemon juice

Salt

60 g (½ cup) diced pitted dates

37 g (¼ cup) slivered almonds

DAY 1

To make the crust, in a medium bowl, whisk together the flour and salt. Add the lard and rub the mixture with your fingertips. Using a pastry blender or two butter knives, cut the butter into the mixture until it resembles coarse crumbs.

In a small bowl, combine the lemon juice, egg and sourdough discard. Add this mixture to the flour and stir until it's just combined. Add the water 14 grams (1 tablespoon) at a time, just until the dough begins to clump together. Bring the dough together using your hands, then wrap it in plastic wrap and refrigerate overnight.

To make the filling, in a small bowl, mix the ginger, cinnamon and turmeric. Rub the spices all over the chicken breast, place it in an airtight container and refrigerate for at least 30 minutes.

Heat the oil in a medium skillet over medium heat and fry the chicken for 2 minutes on each side. Transfer to a plate. Add the onion to the skillet and sauté until it's soft, about 2 minutes. Return the chicken to the skillet and add the stock. Bring to a simmer, cover and simmer for 30 minutes, or until the chicken is cooked through and tender. Remove the mixture from the heat and shred the chicken. Return the skillet with the shredded chicken to the heat and reduce the cooking liquid by simmering for about 5 minutes. Add the lemon juice and season with salt. Remove the mixture from the heat and stir in the dates and almonds. Transfer everything to an airtight container and refrigerate overnight.

(Continued)

TOPPING

4 g (1 tsp) ground cinnamon

42 g (3 tbsp) granulated sugar

DAY 2

Preheat the oven to 400°F (200°C). Line an 18 x 13-inch (45 x 33-cm) baking sheet with parchment paper. Set a small bowl of water near your work surface.

Roll out the dough on a lightly floured surface to ⅛-inch (3-mm) thickness. Using a 5-inch (13-cm) biscuit cutter, cut out 10 to 15 disks. Reroll the scraps only once. Place about 7 to 10 grams (2 teaspoons) of filling on each disk. Moisten the edges all around with water and fold the pastry over the filling, so you have a half circle. Seal the edges with a fork. Place the empanadas on the lined baking sheet and refrigerate them for 20 minutes. Bake for 15 minutes, or until the crust is evenly browned.

While they're baking, make the topping. Combine the cinnamon and sugar in a large bowl. As the empanadas come out of the oven, use tongs to toss them in the cinnamon sugar while they are still hot. Then cool them on a wire rack before serving.

Store the empanadas in an airtight container in the refrigerator for up to 3 days.

ACKNOWLEDGMENTS

To Joel, for your love and support, for sharing in all my triumphs and bearing my frustration. Thank you for encouraging my weird hobby, for seeing all that was possible even before I ever could. For never complaining when I turned our home into a test kitchen, and for scrubbing sticky starter from mixing bowls piled high in our sink.

To my family. My loving parents, for raising me with a deep love and appreciation for good food. Thank you for making sacrifices so that I could be free to pursue what I love. To my brother, who tested a number of these recipes and let me see my book through a beginner's eyes. My sister, for teaching me how to make my first batch of oatmeal cookies and igniting my love affair with baking.

To my best friends, Hang, Nancy and Mikia, for their never-ending support and encouragement, for squashing my self-doubt every time it reared its ugly head, and for making me believe that I was capable of achieving everything I set my mind to.

To Gaby, for bringing my vision to life. You've been a true creative partner. Thank you for pouring your love and creativity into this project. For allowing me to have unlimited retakes whenever I thought the bakes didn't look perfect, and for being the taste tester for all the recipes in the book.

To my editor, Jenna, and the Page Street Publishing team. Thank you for giving me guidance, seeing my potential and making my dream of writing a book come true.

To Nicky Giusto and Central Milling, without whom this book would not have been possible. Thank you for supplying me with your beautiful flour, which I used to create and test most of the recipes in this book.

To the online community of sourdough bloggers and bakers who so generously share their knowledge and expertise with the world.

Finally, to all of you who have supported Make It Dough. Thank you for following me on my baking journey and inspiring me to explore the possibilities of sourdough. I know there are plenty of sourdough bloggers out there, so I'm proud that you have chosen to support my blog and that the information I offer provides some value in your own adventure with wild yeasts.

ABOUT THE AUTHOR

Hannah Dela Cruz is a self-taught baker whose love affair with her oven started after she baked a batch of oatmeal cookies with her older sister at the age of ten. She takes pride in her Filipino heritage and upbringing, which imbued her with a deep passion for delicious food. Ever since she got bit by the sourdough bug, she has been obsessed with putting a sourdough twist in everything and anything she cooks and bakes. Hannah started her blog, Make It Dough, in September 2018, and her obsession with sourdough resulted in a *Saveur* Magazine Special Interest Blog Award a year later.

INDEX